DATE DUE

NO 1'00			
NO 27'00			
DE 18 03			
AP 7 04			
AP 20 05			

DEMCO 38-296

THE
BEST
AMERICAN
SHORT
PLAYS
1997-1998

Best American Short Plays Series

THE
BEST
AMERICAN
SHORT
PLAYS
1997-1998

edited by
GLENN YOUNG

NEW YORK • LONDON

THE BEST AMERICAN SHORT PLAYS 1997-1998

No part of this publication may be reproduced or transmitted in any form or by any means, electronic or mechanical, including photocopy, recording, or any information storage or retrieval system now known to be invented, without permission in writing from the publishers, except by a reviewer who wishes to quote brief passages in connection with a review written for inclusion in a magazine, newspaper or broadcast.

NOTE: All plays contained in this volume are fully protected under the Copyright Laws of the United States of America, the British Empire, including the Dominion of Canada, and all other countries of the International Copyright Union and the Universal Copyright Convention. Permission to reproduce, wholly or in part, by any method, must be obtained from the copyright owners or their agents. (See CAUTION notices at the beginning of each play.)

Copyright ©2000 by Applause Theatre Book Publishers
All Rights Reserved
ISBN 1-55783-365-6 (cloth), 1-55783-366-4 (paper)
ISSN 0067-6284

APPLAUSE BOOKS
1841 Broadway, Suite 1100
New York, NY 10023
Phone (212) 765-7880
Fax (212) 765-7875

Combined Book Service Ltd.
Units I/K, Paddock Wood Distribution Centre
Paddock Wood, Tonbridge, Kent
TN12 6UU
Phone (44) 01892 837171
Fax (44) 01892 837272

Printed in Canada

CONTENTS

To Howard and Marianne Stein

Maria Bernhard

Suzannah Blinkoff

Janet Borrus

BELLYFRUIT

Maria Bernhard

Maria Bernhard studied playwriting at the Los Angeles Theatre Centre's Young Playwrights Lab with Mira-Lani Oglesby and later joined their Women Playwrights Lab. In 1991 she won the American College Theatre Festival Award for Best Original One Act Play, *Secret Circus*, which she wrote and directed. That year she also graduated from The Claremont Colleges, where she earned the Curtain Raisers Scholarship, and the Virginia Princehouse Allen Award for distinguished contribution to the theater. She then went on to Europe, where she performed briefly with Circus Archaos in Germany and then formed her own street spectacle, touring from Sweden to Greece as a dancer and juggler.

Maria began teaching dance and drama to middle school students in Watts in 1993 and continued to teach in the Los Angeles Unified School District for the next five years. During that time, she wrote a collection of short stories based on her extraordinary experiences, entitled *Sub in the Hood*, which she hopes to publish soon.

In 1994, she attended the Padua Hills Playwrights Festival, where she studied with Maria Irene Fornes, Murray Mednick and Neena Beber, among others. In 1995, she co-founded the Writer's and Actor's Lab, which presents the work of many esteemed writers and actors. Maria has written three original screenplays and is represented by Infinity Management International. Her latest script, *Michiganders*, she plans to direct herself in the near future. She lives in Hollywood with her husband, musician Still James.

Susannah Blinkoff

Susannah Blinkoff began writing plays in 1989 at Padua Hills Playwrights Festival in Los Angeles, and has also written two original screenplays. She has taught acting to runaway teens on Hollywood Boulevard and to college students at The Chautaqua Institute. In 1993, she founded the Young Mothers Writing Program at El Nido Family Center in Pacoima, California which was the initial inspiration for *Bellyfruit*.

As an actress, she began her professional career in New York Off-Broadway at age twelve. A graduate of Brown University, she has acted on television and in numerous stage productions in New York and Los Angeles, working with such notable directors as Herbert Berghof, Geraldine Fitzgerald, Peter Riegert and Richard Masur. In 1994, she made her Broadway debut in the *The Best Little Whorehouse Goes Public* and was a featured vocalist on the cast album recording. Her one-woman musical *Momma is a Witch* was seen in New York at HERE and in Los Angeles at Lunapark.

Also a singer/songwriter, Susannah performs regularly in Los Angeles at Agape, Martini Lounge, Cafe Largo and The Mint, and has also sung in Galway, Ireland. Her music will be featured in the screenplay adaptation of *Bellyfruit*. She lives in Los Angeles with her husband, director Jordan Corngold.

Janet Borrus

Janet Borrus, an actress for over fifteen years, began writing out of a desire to see more characters on the stage and screen who reflect the cultural variety, emotional complexity, intelligence and strength of women she encounters every day. Her first effort, the one-act *Billy-Ann's Misplaced Her Baby*, was presented in Los Angeles at First Stage. *The Ramona Roses*, a solo show inspired by her experiences teaching at-risk girls at Ramona High School in East Los Angeles, has received high critical acclaim and sparked lively discussion on both sides of the Atlantic. Since premiering in Los Angeles in 1997, it has traveled to Ireland, New York, San Francisco, St. Louis and Santa Fe, and will be presented in India in 1999. Janet is currently working on a screenplay adaptation.

Her other stage credits as an actress included *The Heidi Chronicles*, *What the Butler Saw*, Peter Parnell's *Romance Language*, *Once In A Lifetime*, and the west coast premieres of *Isolate*, *Burrhead*, *Power Video* and many other new plays. She has appeared on numerous television shows and recently made her feature film debut in the screen adaptation of *Bellyfruit*.

A teacher as well, Janet co-created and toured extensively with Shakespeare Unbound, a bilingual program developed for Los Angeles high schools. She also conducts "storymaking" workshops in which she guides participants through dramatization of stories from their own lives. She is a graduate of Oberlin College and The London Drama Studio.

Maria Bernhard, Susannah Blinkoff and Janet Borrus also collaborated on the screenplay adaptation of *Bellyfruit*, which was filmed in Los Angeles in 1998. The feature-length film, directed by Kerri Green, was produced by Bonnie Dickenson and Robert Bauer for Independent Women Artists.

CHARACTERS

SHANIKA, female, age 14, African-American

ARACELY, female, age 15, Latina

CHRISTINA, female, age 16, Caucasian

JIMMY, male, late 20's, African-American, gangbanger

TOYA, female, age 8, younger sister of Shanika

ARLENE, female, mid-30's, Christina's mother

KARLA, female, age 15, Aracely's cousin

OSCAR, male, age 19, mechanic, Aracely's boyfriend

CHORUS #1, female, African-American, plays teenage mom, nurse

CHORUS #2, female, Caucasian, plays teenage mom, nurse, Aracely's mother [*O.S.* voice], stranger

CHORUS #3, female, Latina, plays teenage mom, nurse, guy at party

This production can be performed by as few as 6 actors and as many as 16.

Translation of all Spanish words follows the text.

All rights to the song "*Rockabye*" are owned by Susannah Blinkoff copyright 1996. Sheet music available upon request.

[*Sound of a school bell ringing. A chorus of six teenage girls addresses the audience.*]

SHANIKA: He said if we did it standin' up, it wouldn't get me this way.

ARACELY: I thought it would be all romantic, you know, like in the *novelas* on T.V.

CHRISTINA: You know how you can only get pregnant like two days out of the month? That's when I took the pill!

ALL: You lay and play, you gotta pay!

CHORUS #3: Before I had my baby, I did some modeling at the mall, but they don't call me no more.

CHORUS #1: They gave out condoms at school but I don't like to mess with no Jimmy when we gettin' busy.

CHORUS #2: When I was thirteen, I had big ones.

CHORUS #3: My homeboys are cool. We go out drinking and they never let me pay 'cause I got a kid.

CHORUS #2: When I was fourteen, I had big ones.

CHORUS #1: I want to name my baby Trayvon — how do you spell that?

CHORUS #2: When I was fifteen, I had my baby and now I have huge ones.

CHORUS #3: It's cool 'cause I'm pregnant, my mom's pregnant and my *abuela's* pregnant too. We're all having babies at the same time.

SHANIKA: My mom was 16 when she had me. I'm 14. So I guess it just runs in the family.

ARACELY: You know how it is. He just kept saying the right things.

CHRISTINA: I wasn't thinking about having a baby when I was having sex. I was thinking about having *sex* when I was having sex...

ALL: [*Joining in.*]...like most people, right?

[*School bell rings. The chorus exits. Lights up on* SHANIKA *sitting on her front stoop in the housing projects.*]

SHANIKA: Jimmy ran up to me yesterday and said he just killed someone. We sat down on my front steps and watched the police surround the projects. They didn't find the guns. He said he threw one in the trash and one up on the roof. Be a lotta guns up on them roofs. Too scared to use the same one twice. He was sweating like a motherfucker but they din' never ask us no questions. We just sat there, my big old belly stickin' out. Pregnant girl, pregnant girl, they think I don't know nothin' 'cause I'm fulla fruit. Well, this ain't no mango, papaya, beachball, officer, this is a baby in here so you know I cain't be all that innocent.

[*Lights crossfade to* CHRISTINA *in the modest apartment that she shares with her mother.*]

CHRISTINA: I had sex with seven guys last Saturday. Not many girls can say that. See, I decided not to feel bad about who I am and just accept that I'm a slut. It's what I am. You don't always get to choose what you are. I tried to change. It doesn't work. Last weekend I went to a party with my best friend. I was gonna be this whole new person, right? I wasn't gonna just get wasted and go off with some guy. But as soon as her boyfriend showed up she ditched me. Then practically everybody started pairing up, and I just kind of stood there feeling...stupid. Then I saw this whole other group of guys sitting on the wall. And they were all looking at me.

[*Lights crossfade to* ARACELY *outside her high school.*]

ARACELY: I think I saw Jesus this morning. I got off the bus near the church over there on Breed Street and I was feeling really bad. I was depressed, you know? And then I turned around and I seen this man. He had long red, like, brownish hair, he had a beard, and blue eyes. He looked like a photo that people say is God. And when I looked at him, he told me "Don't cry, my child." And just like suddenly all the tears in me went away and the ugly feeling in me went away. It was the most beautifulest feeling! And when I turned back to ask him who he was, he wasn't there no more. It was like a sudden gone thing.

SHANIKA: Jimmy and me look good sittin' there together and he was actin' all sweet and shit, I almost forget he just shoot somebody. He kiss my cheek and thank me for hangin' with him an' he go back to playin' dice. Then my baby kicked me and I went back inside. Ain't nowhere else to go. Can't go to the park no more 'cause a funny man grabs girls asses there. I didn't feel like watchin' T.V. so I just lay on the couch and looked at my big bellyfruit, ripening every minute. Brown sparkling fruit with green apple eyes.

CHRISTINA: They started calling me "sexy girl" and "beautiful." It made me feel good. I took off this sweater I had on over this kind of crop top thing. I downed one of their beers and started making out with one of them. Then, somehow, I was sitting on one of the other guy's laps and...then everything got really wild.

ARACELY: You know, I been praying a lot. Nobody talks in my family no more. My mom lost her job and my dad, well, he just don't talk. By the time he gets home, it's late and he just turns on the T.V. and don't say nothing. My brother's always kicking it with his girlfriend...and, like, I don't have nobody. And my skin's still so *nasty*. People say be happy with yourself, but...I don't know how.

SHANIKA: While I was waitin' for my mama to come home, Jimmy shot somebody else and still didn't get caught. Three shots to the boy's head. Them homeboys shoulda covered his face, shouldn't make his mama see his face all tore up like that. They say you just have to keep your eyes shut...Somebody said it was over a welfare check, but when they looked in his pockets, nigguh only had two dollars.

CHRISTINA: The guys took me to a park. I tried to run but I was in the middle of this mass of men. At first, I was scared but then there was nothing I could do. They were all undressing me and undressing themselves, grabbing at me and...I don't really remember. Anyway, that's it. I did them all. Not many girls can say they did what I did.

ARACELY: And like this morning on the bus, I was thinking "Oh, I just hate myself and I could just end my life and never have a life again," you know? And then, I seen that man. And I think if I could see him again, he could help me straighten up my life and get back on track, 'cause I'm not there all the way. And I don't know if it was Jesus or God, but I just pray to whoever it was to help me get better, and not worry no more, and to be happy like everybody else, and not be sad.

SHANIKA: A nightmare is the thing you dream that's worse than the thing you see when you wake up, right?

[*Blackout.*]

[*Lights up on* ARACELY *and her cousin* KARLA *in* KARLA'S *bedroom. The radio plays in the backround. The two girls sit on a pink bedspread, surrounded by stuffed animals, applying makeup.*]

KARLA: Look, Cuz, my mom got me a Christmas bear.

[KARLA *grabs a stuffed animal and shows it to* ARACELY. ARACELY *grabs another one from the pile on the bed.*]

ARACELY: *Ay*, they're *novios!*

KARLA: Let's get them married.

[*They hum the wedding march.*]

ARACELY: Do you, Alfredo Bear, take Lady Bear to be your lawful wedded bear, to have and to hold, 'til death do you part?

KARLA: *Si*. And do you, Lady Bear, take Alfredo Bear to be your lawfully wedded bear, to have and to hold, to love and to cherish, to hug and to kiss, 'til death do you part?

ARACELY: *Con toda mi corazon.*

KARLA: Okay, now we kiss.

[*They make the bears kiss.*]

KARLA: [*Continuing.*] Okay, now we have kids.

ARACELY: *Ay*, so fast!

ARACELY'S MOTHER: [*Offstage.*] Aracely, we have to pick up *Papi* or he'll get mad!

ARACELY: He's mad all the time anyways. I gotta go. I wish you didn't move so far away.

KARLA: Me, too. *Adios*, Celi.

ARACELY: *Luego.*

ARACELY'S MOTHER: *Mi'ja!*

ARACELY: *Ay, vengo!*

[*Lights crossfade to* SHANIKA.]

SHANIKA: I know some sick people. My brother-in-law used to abuse me sexually, like every night, so I started stayin' at my cousin Brandy's so I could just go to sleep, no worries, you know. The last time I was there, Brandy asked me do I want the night light on and me bein' afraid of the dark, I said yep. Ten minutes later, the night light went off and Brandy was comin' toward me and she grabbed me real tight and I said, "Whatchoo want?" and she goes, "You." After she did her thing, I laid there shakin' all night. Now, I'm never in the dark with anyone, not even my closest friends and family 'cause you just can't tell if a person's sick in the head.

[*Lights crossfade to* CHRISTINA.]

CHRISTINA: I slept in the bathtub last night. I watched this really scary movie about two sisters and one is really evil and the other one is in a wheelchair. It freaked me out so bad, I had to sleep in the bathroom 'cause it's the only door in the house that has a lock. My mom's been gone four days this time…'sposed to be just the weekend. She usually calls, unless she's really drunk. I hope she's OK. She's fine. Guess she got lucky. Whatever. I don't care, I just wish she'd left me some money. They turned the gas off on Friday so I'm, like, wearing six sweaters. But it's not a tragedy or anything. We have a microwave.

[*Lights crossfade to* SHANIKA's *bedroom, where she lies half-dressed with her boyfriend* JIMMY.]

JIMMY: Why you gotta get so mad, baby? I'm just tryin' to take it to another level.

SHANIKA: It's just — I just wanted it to be nicer.

JIMMY: Baby, I'm bein' as nice as I can be.

SHANIKA: No, you ain't. You just being however you wanna be without asking me what do I want.

JMMY: Baby, you act like you like it.

SHANIKA: No, I don't and you don't even notice when I tell you to slow down or nothin'. You actin' just like my cousin —

JIMMY: Man, I ain't even like that pervert!

SHANIKA: You think you gotta just get in there and you forget it's me. Why y'all gotta treat me like shit!

JIMMY: Man, I don't even know what's goin' on. You actin' like a little baby. You best hang out with your teddy bear, girl, 'cause I ain't into this. You got some serious problems —

SHANIKA: YOU the one got problems, Jimmy! YOU the one got problems! Where you goin', man? Jimmy, come back...

[*Lights crossfade to* CHRISTINA *and her mother* ARLENE *in the bathroom of their apartment.*]

ARLENE: Why'd you have to lock the bathroom door? I thought you overdosed or slit your wrists or something.

CHRISTINA: Not yet.

ARLENE: Don't start. God, I need coffee.

CHRISTINA: Good luck. The gas got turned off.

ARLENE: They said I had 'til the end of the month! Shit, I was gonna pay it, I just needed cash this weekend. [*Sighs.*] I'm a lousy mother, right?

CHRISTINA: [*Reciting her usual response.*] No, you're not.

ARLENE: C'mon, I'll take us out to breakfast.

CHRISTINA: I have school, Mom.

ARLENE: I haven't seen you all weekend, I want to tell you about Frank. I need advice.

CHRISTINA: Frank? What happened to Gary?

ARLENE: Gary is an asshole. Frank's the one.

CHRISTINA: Did you tell him about me?

ARLENE: Frank needs more time to fall in love with me but soon I'll tell him all about you. Then you'll have a father.

CHRISTINA: I don't want a father.

ARLENE: You want the bills paid?

[*Lights crossfade to* ARACELY, *lying on her bed, writing a letter.*]

ARACELY: Dear Cuz, last night my new boyfriend Oscar took me home and I was singing to him and I was naked. I can't believe I'm telling you this but I got to tell somebody. This is the happiest day of my life. I met him at the car show. There were all these hoochie girls there. Then I walk by and he goes, "Hey, *guapa.*" His eyes are *so* green! Last night, he took me to the beach. They have all shops and restaurants and everybody is walking with their man and their babies and buying things and looking *nice.* Then we went back to the apartment he shares with this guy Lucky and he put on that song "*Baby I'm For Real.*" *Ay,* I love that song so much and I love him so much, I started singing…Then he told me to take off my clothes and keep singing…and so I did and then…It was like in a movie! He is the most sexiest man I know. I got home really late but I ain't tired. I know we're gonna get married someday. He don't even look at hoochie girls no more. Don't tell nobody 'cause I don't want no *chisme* going around that I'm a 'ho'. My life is all beautiful ever since I been seeing him.

Love,

Your cousin in *love*

[*Blackout.*]

[*Lights up on six teenage girls. A popular r&b love song plays.*]

CHRISTINA: He was different. Way different than some other guys I've been with. He was more…intense.

SHANIKA: "Ooh, I never made love like this before, baby."

ARACELY: He's like…he's like a man. Not like those boys, you know?

CHORUS #2: So one night, I go:

CHORUS #3: "How much do you love me?"

CHORUS #2: And he goes:

CHORUS #1: "A lot."

CHORUS #2: And I go:

CHORUS #3: "How much do you love me?"

CHORUS #2: And he looks at me real serious and says:

CHORUS #1: "I love you, honey. You are the girl that I see bein' my wife and you are the girl I want to have my baby."

ALL: Whoa, he really IS different!

CHORUS #3 I was only fourteen, you know…I was thinking —

CHORUS #2: That I'd go to college someday and maybe —

CHORUS #1: — go to Europe. But when this guy —

ALL: who I loved so much

CHORUS #2: Said those words to me about what HE saw happening —

CHORUS #3: It was like

ALL: Yeah!

CHORUS #1: Yeah, that's what I want!

CHORUS #3: That's what I want to do.

CHORUS #2: I wanna grow your baby inside me. And also, then if we get married —

CHORUS #1 We're a family.

CHRISTINA: And so we did more than kiss. And so…it happened. I had his baby.

ARACELY: I had his baby.

SHANIKA: My baby.

ALL: That's what *real* love is.

[*Blackout.*]

[*Lights up on* ARACELY *praying in her bedroom.*]

ARACELY: Dear Jesus, I been looking for you by Breed Street but you ain't been there. I know it's a blessing to be a mother, but my dad's gonna throw me out when he hears. I know it. Oscar says as soon as he saves some up we'll get our own place but I can't wait that long. I barely fit in my jeans today. My mom's been asking me what am I eating I gained so much weight. And my teacher knows I been sick first period. I'm scared. Please send me a sign that I'm going in the right way.

[*Lights crossfade to* CHRISTINA *in her bathroom.*]

CHRISTINA: It's been three months now and I know. I haven't been to the doctor yet, but I don't have to have a doctor tell me what I can feel. My butt's getting bigger and my boobs — Like, storing up fat for some future time, like I'm some kind of eskimo or something. And I haven't told anyone yet. Sometimes I want to tell like a total stranger on the bus. Or sometimes I just wanna pull up my sweatshirt in front of my mom and her new boyfriend and yell: "Surprise!" No one has any idea. I still go to parties and stuff but I wear really baggy clothes so nobody notices. I even pretended I was on acid so people would still know I'm cool. [*She lights up a cigarette.*] I don't know which guy it was. But it doesn't really matter. It's not like any of these guys are gonna help me out at all. But, you know, a lot of women are alone when they're having a baby, so I'll be just like them. I don't think I'd want any of those guys around anyway. I mean, they're not *fathers*, they're just guys. They were just having sex. Like I was.

[*Lights crossfade to* SHANIKA, *alone outside.*]

SHANIKA: My baby is due in two months. I'm gonna be a fourteen year old mother. I din' eat no apple seeds, din' hold no kitten or puppy, but my belly grows anyway. Jimmy said if we did it

standin' up like, it wouldn't get me this way. He said it would-
n't happen, wouldn't happen 'cause we just met and we ain't in
love yet and all that so this was just for fun, like, just for the hell
of it, baby. But I thought he was IT, you know, a man. I wanted
love. I did. And I got this.

[*Blackout.*]

[*Lights up on* ARACELY *with* CHORUS #1, 2, *and* 3, *dressed in
Nurse's uniforms. The dialogue is rapid, almost overlapping.*]

CHORUS #3: On Monday, go to Planned Parenthood. Their walk-
up hours are 9:30 to 11:30 a.m., then they break for lunch —

CHORUS #1: — and re-open from 1:30 to 3:30 p.m.

ARACELY: That's during school hours.

CHORUS #3: They will do a urine test and if necessary, a blood
test —

CHORUS #2: — for fifteen dollars.

ARACELY: I don't have that.

CHORUS #1: You will then be examined by a doctor who will then
ask how you want to proceed. If you want to abort —

CHORUS #3: — they will schedule an appointment for the next day.
If you are not on Medi-Cal —

ARACELY: The next day?

CHORUS #2: — this will cost two hundred-seventy-five dollars under local anesthesia, three hundred-seventy-five under a general —

ARACELY: That's almost four hundred dollars!

CHORUS #3: If you cannot afford this, you must get on Medi-Cal.

CHORUS #1: To get on Medi-Cal, ask the examining physician for a
note saying that you require a therapeutic abortion.

ARACELY: A what?

CHORUS #3: You then take this to the Medi-Cal office.

CHORUS #2: Between the hours of 7 a.m. and 3 p.m.

ARACELY: I don't have a car.

CHORUS #1: Get there early in the morning.

CHORUS #2: On the application, check the box for "Emergency."

CHORUS #3: Remember to file as an independent because if there are five people in your family —

CHORUS #1: — with a combined monthly income of one thousand two hundred fifty-nine dollars —

CHORUS #3: You are ineligible.

ARACELY: Wait a minute —

CHORUS #2: You will also need to show Medi-Cal the doctor's note and you must leave it there, so be sure to make a xerox copy before you go.

CHORUS #3: Your application will take at least three days to process.

ARACELY: I thought you said one day.

CHORUS #1: Before you leave the Medi-Cal office, be sure to ask them how soon you can return to pick up your card.

CHORUS #2: You must have your card when you return to Planned Parenthood.

ARACELY: That's four buses!

CHORUS #3: Make sure someone accompanies you home.

CHORUS #1: Follow doctor's instructions regarding rest and activity.

[*Lights out on* CHORUS. *Spotlight on* ARACELY.]

ARACELY: Yeah, I was gonna go to Planning Parenthood, but I'm gonna have it now...I felt it kick.

[ARACELY *and* CHORUS #3 *exit.*]

[*Lights shift to* CHRISTINA *with* CHORUS MEMBERS *#1 and #2.*]

CHRISTINA: At the hospital, everyone kept asking me about the father.

CHORUS #1: Who's the father?

CHORUS #2: Where's your boyfriend?

CHORUS #1 Lucky guy...

CHORUS #2: Are you gonna get married?

CHORUS #1: What does he do?

CHORUS #2: What name does he like?

CHORUS #1: So when's the wedding?

CHRISTINA: They gave me all these forms to fill out and all the real fathers it could be just blurred in my head: the guys on the field, that boy from Spanish class, my friend's brother, the guy at the 7-11...and I just started crying. This nurse came up to me and asked me what was wrong and I told her I didn't know and she said:

CHORUS #2: What? What don't you know?

CHRISTINA: And I said, "I don't know who the father is!" I felt so stupid. Like, yeah, I'm really popular now, right? So she says:

CHORUS #1: You can get the different men to come in for a test ...

CHRISTINA: — and I'm, like, picturing the guys at my school. No way am I gonna go up to, like, thirty different guys and say, "Hi! I don't know if this is your kid, but if you could just come down to the hospital for a test..." And then I realized I don't even like any of them and that was too depressing. So I told the nurse that the father moved out of state and I don't know where he is. And she said:

CHORUS #2: Oh, I see.

CHRISTINA: And wrote "Unknown" in about a million places on the page. Sometimes I feel like I made a really big mistake...

[CHRISTINA *and* CHORUS #1 *and* #2 *exit.*]

[*Lights up on* SHANIKA, *alone, nine months pregnant.*]

SHANIKA: Sometimes people look at me and they got this *ex-pres-sion*. It's like, "Ohh, that poor nigger and pregnant, too, what a shame." Well I say, look man, this ain't a crime. I din' shoot nobody, I ain't no gangster, I ain't down with no crack. This a baby in here. It's not a bomb. It's gonna be a person. Why they be lookin' at me all sorry and shit? I'm doin' the most highest thing a female can do. So don't look at me with pity. I got pride. You should *re-spect* me. I'm gonna be a mother. It don't matter how old I am. Being a mom's the best thing a woman can be. It's beautiful. I'm beautiful. And my baby's gon' be beautiful, too. So stop lookin' at me like that.

[SHANIKA *turns on her heel and exits.* ARACELY *enters, carrying her baby in her arms.*]

ARACELY: I woke up with this strange pain seventeen minutes apart. I didn't eat nothing the whole day. The next day, the pain got every five minutes. My aunt gave me a tea and one hour after that, the pain got every two minutes. My body felt like it had chili juice instead of blood. I blacked out. I seen a light, I pray "God, please, if you want to take me, just let me hold my baby once before I die." Then I'm dreaming that I'm at his funeral. He's in a little tiny white coffin. I'm looking and looking but I can't see his face because I don't know what he looks like yet. I yell, "Let me see him, let me see him, turn him over!" Then I blacked out again. Four hours later, I finally got to hold him.

[CHRISTINA *enters, holding her baby in her arms.*]

CHRISTINA: I have a huge scar. It's really gross. They had to cut me open 'cause the baby came five weeks too early. I felt like I was in a magic trick, you know, like I was the girl inside the box with everybody watching while the guy saws me in half. They cut my stomach open! Like I will ever wear a crop top again, right? But then the nurse…she puts this little wet person on my chest and I could see these little fingernails and toes, her little ear was right over my heart and then she opened up these blue *amazing* eyes and looked right at me. She's the most incredible and per-fect thing I've ever seen! And she came out of me…which proves I'm not as fucked up as I thought, you know?

[*Blackout.*]

[*Lights up on* SHANIKA'S *boyfriend* JIMMY, *outside the hospital.*]

JIMMY: I don't care what y'all say, birth is a motherfuckin' act of God, it's a miracle, okay. I just saw my son. I wanted to put out my hands, you know, and hold that little body, but when I think of all the shit I done with 'em, I couldn't even touch him. I ain't good. I WAS good, we all good when we startin' out, but I went down the wrong path and the last thing I want is for my son to follow me. I ain't no example. But I din' get one neither. Look, I don't know how's a father's 'sposed to be, but I ain't no father. Maybe someday, I'll come around, you know, change and shit, but I don't know. You know what though? He look like me, my son. I like that. What a day, man. I'm never gon' forget seein' him pop out. Most amazing thing I ever seen, and I seen a lotta things, lotta things.

[JIMMY *exits.*]

[*Lights up on teenage girls. School bell rings. The girls speak as if reading a school assignment.*]

ALL: "How My Life Changed After My Baby Was Born."

CHORUS #3: Instead of buying makeup, I buy Pampers.

CHORUS #2: I gained weight.

CHORUS #1: I lost weight.

ARACELY: I gained a lot of weight.

ALL: My body changed a LOT..

SHANIKA: Can't sleep, have to wake up in the middle of the night.

CHORUS #3: Six a.m., get him up, give him a bath.

CHRISTINA: Left school for a while and got behind.

ARACELY: I got overprotected and learned how to drive.

CHORUS #2: I have to not only take care of my baby but also my boyfriend.

ALL: I have to be responsible.

CHORUS #1: My boyfriend has to drive more careful, he hates to go slow.

SHANIKA: Me and the baby's dad, we separated.

ARACELY: My boyfriend and me are tired, we fight a lot.

CHORUS #3: I feel uncomfortable having sex with my boyfriend.

ARACELY: It's not romantic anymore.

ALL: We don't have sex.

CHORUS #1: There's less time for ourselves.

CHORUS #2: I can't go out!

CHRISTINA: I use up all my money on my kid.

SHANIKA: I have to do a lotta laundry.

ARACELY: I have a lotta stains.

CHRISTINA: It's hard to pick up guys when you smell like diapers.

ALL: I can't date at all!

CHORUS #3: I can't wear little skirts no more.

CHORUS #2: I can't curse as much.

CHORUS #1: I lost my friends.

SHANIKA: I didn't really have a childhood.

ALL: I didn't really have a childhood.

[*Blackout.*]

[*Lights up on three separate playing areas:* CHRISTINA *and* GUY AT THE PARTY, SHANIKA *and* TOYA *and* ARACELY *on the phone. A rap radio station plays in the background. Whoever has focus is in brighter light, with others in tableau.*]

[SHANIKA *sits on her front stoop holding her baby, watching* TOYA *dance and move her hips in sync with the rhythm of a playground chant.*]

TOYA: Penny, penny, nickel, dime, show me yours, I'll show you mine!

SHANIKA: Girl, where'd you learn that?

TOYA: Penny, penny, nickel, dime, if you want me, stand in line!

SHANIKA: You better knock that off!

[SHANIKA *tries to grab* TOYA *but the baby in her arms makes it impossible. Toya starts again, dancing sexily.*]

TOYA: Dime, dime, quarter, dollar, if you like me, stand and holler Hey, Ho, Hey, Ho ...

[*Lights shift to* CHRISTINA *with* PARTY GUY. *He drinks and smokes while she shows him photographs. She has to shout over the music.*]

CHRISTINA: Oh my god, my breast milk makes her shit, like really liquid, right? And last night, I was changing her and it squirted in my face! It was so disgusting! But she's *so* cute! I won't date a guy unless he likes babies so...do you like 'em?

[PARTY GUY *looks at the photo, then at* CHRISTINA, *then exits.*]

[*Lights shift to* ARACELY *in her kitchen talking to* KARLA *on the telephone over the music.*]

ARACELY: Cuz, hi...yeah, it's me. How ya been? Did you call last week? Our phone got disconnected and...oh, I thought you mighta called. Uh...I'm okay —

[*Shouting to the next room.*]

Lucky, *baja la musica* !

[*The radio music stops.*]

ARACELY: [*Cont'd.*] Oh, yeah...Francisco's beautiful, he's my little angel. Thank your mom for the little sweater, it's perfect. How's school?...Oh, yeah, congratulations! My mom told me you won some contest...You get to go camping? Wow, that's great. I miss school...Nah, I don't know when I'm going back yet. I don't have nobody to watch the baby. My mom's working again. Yeah, she came by last week. It was nice but then she cried and I just wanted her to leave...LUCKY! *Ay*, he put his stupid cigarette out in Francisco's bottle. THESE BOTTLES ARE EXPENSIVE, LUCKY! He's leaving soon anyway, we're kicking him out...Oscar's okay, he's out looking for a job. Wait, my call waiting. Yeah? Hello? Oscar, where are you?...What did you do ?...LUCKY, OSCAR'S LOCKED UP!
[*Blackout.*]

[*Lights up on* ARLENE *in apartment.* CHRISTINA *enters, slightly drunk, to find* ARLENE *holding the baby in one arm and mixing herself a drink with her free hand.*]

ARLENE: You're forty minutes late, Christina! We agreed that you'd be home by —

CHRISTINA:Hi, baby! Hi, sweetie, did you miss me?

ARLENE: Shhh! She finally just fell asleep.

[ARLENE *gives the baby to* CHRISTINA.]

ARLENE: [*Continued.*] What, you can't tell time?

CHRISTINA: The party rocked and no one wanted to leave! I couldn't get a ride —

ARLENE: She cried and screamed all night. She drove me crazy.

CHRISTINA: She cried for me? Ohhh, you missed me, little sweetie, didn't you. Well, mommy won't leave you ever again, I promise.

ARLENE: Right. Not 'til there's another rockin' party.

CHRISTINA: I'm just trying to meet someone, okay? Sound familiar?

ARLENE: It's not that easy, trust me. I gave up everything when I had you! Everything!

CHRISTINA: So I was forty minutes late, so what, mom! Don't shit lightning bolts.

ARLENE: You don't get it, do you? I am not your babysitter! I already DID this, I raised you all by myself for sixteen years!

CHRISTINA: Mom —

ARLENE: No, Christina! You got pregnant, not me! This is your mess, not mine!

[ARLENE *exits.*]

[CHRISTINA *cuddles the baby and coos.*]

CHRISTINA: You're not a mess, you're beautiful. Grandma's just a bitch.

[*Lights crossfade to* ARACELY *and her boyfriend* OSCAR.]

OSCAR: Hey, 'Cely, I brought you some money for Francisco. A hundred dollars. And I'm gonna bring you more next week. I'm working steady now, down at Vega's, helper to the main mechanic. Barely two months out — My parole officer says he never seen a guy come back so fast...I wanna be with you again, babe. I wanna see my boy. I been showing everyone his picture and it gets to me, you know? I wanna hold him. I wanna hold you. You're lookin' *fine* ... I ain't been drinkin'. Ain't been messin' with my homeboys. I ain't even been smokin' weed. I'm in a program now. I got it under control, babe. I got respect for myself now. And I'm gonna be up. And I can help you be up. I'll work, you can go back to school. Make a family, you know? Let me kiss you, eh?

[*He tries to kiss her. She hesitates.*]

OSCAR: [*Continuing.*] Oscar's for reals, you know. We're gonna be UP.

[*He draws her in for a kiss and they walk off together.*]

[*Lights shift to* SHANIKA, *holding a bag of groceries, with* CHORUS #1.]

SHANIKA: Jimmy is out, okay? He din' bring me a fuckin' dime. Soon as I had the baby, he was gone. I ran out of money so I went downtown to get some food. Have you ever tried to get food from the county? It's not like you just walk down the street and, boom, they give you a sack fulla groceries. No, girl, they got you fillin' out more paperwork than I ever saw in school. Half the shit you don't even know what they're talkin' about and you have to bring in electric bills and letters from your landlord and all this...I mean, can't they tell when you hungry? Then, at the end of the day, I had to listen to some lady tellin' me how to cook proper. I'm like, yeah, bitch, you gonna fix my oven? Finally, we got some food. I was so fuckin' hungry by then, I made three sandwiches on the bus home. All I know is, it's easy gettin' pregnant, but everything come after that is so damn hard.

[*Blackout.*]

[*The three* CHORUS MEMBERS *enter.*]

CHORUS #2: I miss school. I never thought I would, but I do.

CHORUS #3: I can't believe my mom let me do whatever I wanted. I'm gonna be strict with *my* kid.

CHORUS #1: All I do with my baby is watch T.V. We never go out or nothin'.

CHORUS #2: No guys go out with you if you have a kid.

CHORUS #3: I go for every job I hear about, but they all say the same thing. "What if your kid gets sick? We can't depend on you."

CHORUS #1: When she's 16 I'll be 30. That's not too old to go to college. Is it?

[*The* CHORUS *exits.*]

[*Lights up on* CHRISTINA *with her baby, knocking on an apartment door.*]

CHRISTINA: Hi, um, I'm Christina and this is my daughter and, uh…we're kinda stuck. John lets us stay here sometimes. I can't stay with my mom 'cause her new boyfriend can't deal with the baby crying, he gets migraines and he's pissed off 'cause I borrowed some money without asking. I was gonna tell him. Anyway, I went to this shelter place in Hollywood but I could only stay two weeks. And then I slept in this van with a guy and his girlfriend and their baby but it was really crowded and then they got lice and…I mean, I'm not, like, homeless. I'm not gonna end up to be one of those people who gets their baby taken away by the county. I'm a normal person! I was popular, okay? But now it's like…we don't even have a place to sleep. Aren't people supposed to *like* babies?

[*Lights shift to* ARACELY.]

ARACELY: Oscar's in jail again. I don't know if I can wait for him this time. Francisco keeps asking, "Where's Daddy? Where's Daddy?" So yesterday I brought him to see Oscar during visiting hours and Francisco reached out to try to touch him and the glass got in his way, and that's what gets me. I'm *mad*. I'm so *mad* that I have to bring him to see his daddy in jail and tell him to wave "Hi, Daddy" through this glass! I don't want him to grow up with a picture of his daddy as a criminal and have that on him for the rest of his life. Do you think he'll remember? Do you think he'll remember that he saw his daddy in jail?

[*Lights shift to* SHANIKA.]

SHANIKA: My mom got evicted and I had to move in with this guy even though he wasn't the father. At first, he brought me all kinda clothes and food and ice creams and I'm like "Damn, you so sweet." But then one day he comes home and says "I'm sicka that thing cryin' I don't want it around no more, find some other place to live, girl." That's when I saw how it was MY baby, you know, and how nobody wants to take care of some other dude's kid. They all be wantin' they own kid or that's what they say. But what about THIS one, you know? It's like they think the baby don't understand. Well, you understand when somebody don't want you. It's like the sun's gone down and won't never come up.

[*Blackout.*]

Lights up on entire cast for the song "*Rockabye.*"

[*Verses can be divided as befits each cast. Ideally, the three main girls would sing one verse each and sing the chorus together.*]

ROCKABYE

Told my boyfriend he's gonna be a father
He muttered a curse and stood up
Put his boot through the wall, made a nice lookin' hole
Turned on his heel and went out for a stroll
Now he's somewhere drinkin' and I'm awake thinkin'

I gotta do the best that I know

[*Chorus:*]

— Rockabye, I'm gonna try to be better
— Rockabye baby, I've got to be strong
— Don't know why, but I'm doin' what I have to

— Don't cry, baby, we'll get along

Stand at the bus stop, sky starts to rain
I'm balancing the baby on my hip,
It's cold and it's wet and she's startin' to cry
When I'm lookin' for her bottle, the bus passes by
Now we're late for school and I'm covered in drool
I gotta do the best that I know

[*Chorus:*]

— Rockabye, I'm gonna try to be better
— Rockabye baby, I've got to be strong
— Time flies when you're doin' what you have to
— Don't cry, baby, we'll get along

[*Bridge:*]

— We'll be alright, you'll see
— I know what to do
— Have faith in me, baby,
— Momma is countin' on you

She laughs when she runs, she knows twenty-three words
She's growin' as fast as a plant
In my dreams, she makes choices that I never had
And I see her free, honest and glad
Maybe someday, it'll happen that way
'Cause I'm doing the best that I know

[*Chorus:*]

— Rockabye, you will do better
— Rockabye baby, we're growin' strong
— Together, we do what we have to
— And I promise...we'll get along ...
— My baby...we'll get along ...
— I promise...we'll get along
— Rockabye ...
— Rockabye ...
— Rockabye my baby ...
— I promise ...

[*Lights shift.*]

CHRISTINA: I look into my baby's eyes and I see how innocent she is. She doesn't expect the worst from everybody...and I'm gonna keep it that way.

ARACELY: Love isn't all romance. It's a lot of work...And *that's* for reals.

CHORUS #2: Sometimes I wish I was a virgin instead of a mother.

CHORUS #1: Without a man, they call you a single parent.

CHORUS #3: But if you got a man, then you're a family.

SHANIKA: I used to think, like, everything is temporary, you know, don't nothin' last...but now that I have my kid it's just like my mama said:

CHRISTINA: People come and go, but children are forever.

ARACELY: Forever.

ALL: Forever.

[*Blackout.*]

END OF PLAY

TRANSLATIONS:

novela — short for *telenovela*, a serialized drama on television

Ay — the Spanish equivalent of the Yiddish "*oy*"

abuela — grandmother

Papi — father

novios — betrothed, sweethearts

"*con toda mi corazon*" — with all my heart

luego — later

mi'ja — my daughter

"*Ay, vengo*" — alright, I'm coming

guapa — pretty

chisme — gossip

"*baja la musica*" — turn the music down

Steve Feffer

LITTLE AIRPLANES OF THE HEART

The little airplanes of the heart
with their brave little propellers
What can they do
against the winds of darkness
even as butterflies are beaten back
by hurricanes
yet do not die

— Lawrence Ferlinghetti

Steve Feffer

Little Airplanes of the Heart was developed at the Nantucket Short Play Festival and produced at the 1997 Jersey Voices Festival.

Steve's play *The Wizards of Quiz* was developed at the O'Neill National Playwrights Conference, workshopped at Ensemble Studio Theatre, and premiered at the Philadelphia Festival Theatre for New Plays. It was subsequently presented at Chicago's National Jewish Theatre. The play is published by Dramatists Play Service and has been produced at regional, Jewish, college, and community theatres across the country. His play *Marilyn and Marc* was presented by the Victory Gardens Theatre in cooperation with the Shoeless Theatre Company. Steve was a recipient of a new play grant from the Jewish Endowment for the Humanities and the Council of Jewish Theatres for *The Mystery Catcher*, a play based on the life of baseball player/atomic spy Moe Berg. He has received a number of national playwriting awards including the 1997 Dorothy Silver New Jewish Play Award for *Mr. Rebbetzin* which was presented at the American Theatre of Actors. His most recent plays include *Bart, The Temp: A Story of Wall Street*, a contemporary stage version of Melville's *Bartleby*, that has been developed with the Adobe Theatre and the Playwrights Theatre of New Jersey. Steve's theatre pieces appear in Heinemann Books' *Baseball Monologues*, *Elvis Monologues* and *Road Monologues*.

Steve has a Bachelor of Fine Arts degree from New York University in Dramatic Writing, a Master of Fine Arts degree in Playwriting from the University of Iowa Playwrights Workshop, and is currently enrolled in the Ph.D. Program in Theatre and Drama at the University of Wisconsin-Madison. He has taught playwriting and drama at a variety of schools and arts organizations including Young Playwrights Inc. [New York], The Playwrights Theatre of New Jersey, and Rutgers University, and currently, the UW-Madison. He has taught writing and literature at schools that include New York University and Iona College.

Steve lives in historic Cedarburg, Wisconsin with his wife, Cantor Heather Feffer, and a writer's best friend, his golden retriever, Mazel.

CHARACTERS:

UNCLE JOHN, mid 50's.

SAM, John's nephew, age 13.

JILLY, John's daughter, around the same age as Sam.

LORRAINE, Sam's mother.

CHERYL, John's wife.

FARMER JOHN, PRINCIPAL BECKER, and THE RABBI, one male actor.

TIME: *The present.*

PLACE: *The action of the play takes place in* SAM's *house on Cape Cod, MA and in* UNCLE JOHN's *homemade, two seat, single propeller plane, as it flies from Cape Cod to Montana.*

Lights up on UNCLE JOHN. *He is a significantly overweight man in his mid-fifties squeezed into both seats of a homemade, two seat, ultra-light, single propeller plane. The plane is suspended from above the stage over the rest of the action. It remains there for the duration of the play. The plane has been painted bright yellow and says "Cheryl" in small letters on the side.* UNCLE JOHN *wears a scarf, a head set and a leather jacket. Sounds of the plane in flight are heard. Sounds of the wind.* UNCLE JOHN's *scarf is blowing out behind him as he "maneuvers" the plane.*

Lights up on SAM. *He is* UNCLE JOHN's *13 year old nephew. He stands below* UNCLE JOHN's *plane. He holds a small yellow toy plane. He addresses the audience.*

SAM: My Uncle John built an ultra-light airplane. He built it in the basement of our house on Cape Cod and he flew it all the way to a dairy farm in Grassy Butte, North Dakota. Unfortunately he was trying to fly to an airport in Sydney, Montana which was 70 miles further. It was my Uncle John's dream to build a plane and fly it to Montana. [SAM *looks up at* UNCLE JOHN.] Why Montana, Uncle John?

UNCLE JOHN: [*Over the wind and the plane engine.*] Because it's so magnificent.

SAM: But it's 1994. There are roads that go there. Or big jets.

UNCLE JOHN: I know, but it's not the same. Montana is "big sky" country, and it's from outta the big sky that I wanna approach it.

SAM: [*To the audience.*] Uncle John built his plane in our basement because he lived in a ranch house. He thought that building the plane was something that he and his brother, my father, could do. My father never got interested and subsequently he died of a heart attack two years before Uncle John attempted his Montana flight. Everyone in the family thought that it was Uncle John who would die first on account of his weight, but it didn't work out that way. Uncle John had to have the wall of our basement removed so he could get his plane out. "They need to remove the wall to get John out," my mother once joked.

UNCLE JOHN: [*Over the wind and plane noise.*] I thought the plane was something your father and I would fiddle around with — may he rest in peace. But damn if that plane and that state didn't start to get under my skin. Big sky country from outta the big sky. I worked on it a little each day, and before I knew it the plane was finished.

SAM: Other people in the family thought that Uncle John was crazy, but I could spend hours helping him.

[JILLY *enters. She is* UNCLE JOHN's *daughter who is about the same age as* SAM. *She wears a plaid skirt and green blouse that looks like a school uniform.*]

JILLY: My father's crazy, you know?

SAM: No, he's not.

JILLY: Are you going to stay down here all night and watch him?

SAM: I help him.

JILLY: No you don't. You just sit there and watch him. I think maybe you're crazy.

SAM: I'm interested.

JILLY: If you're interested in what a crazy person does, then you must be crazy.

SAM: Uncle John is going to take me with him to Montana because I'm so helpful.

JILLY: Where you gonna fit?

SAM: Uncle John is a genius. He'll find a way.

JILLY: You'd go up in that thing? Now I know you're crazy.

SAM: You won't think we're so crazy when Uncle John and I get to Montana.

JILLY: I'm bored. Come upstairs with me.

SAM: No, thanks.

JILLY: My mother and Auntie Lorraine said that you're supposed to play with me.

SAM: Can't. Gotta help Uncle John.

JILLY: I'll lift up my skirt and show you my underpants if you'll come upstairs and play with me.

SAM: Uncle John's putting on a wing. We got them delivered yesterday in a huge box that took two big men to carry.

JILLY: You really are crazy. [JILLY *lifts up her plaid skirt and shows* SAM *her underpants.*] I see London and I see France. Crazy Cousin Sam can see my underpants.

[JILLY *stands with her skirt up for a beat.* SAM *looks at her confused.*]

UNCLE JOHN: [*Over the wind and airplane noise.*] The first wings that I put on had to be sent back. They weren't big enough on account of all the weight I added to the plane. And, of course, all the weight I had put on.

[UNCLE JOHN *chuckles.*]

But these new wings should do it.

[JILLY *puts her skirt down.*]

JILLY: [*To* UNCLE JOHN.] Why can't you play golf like other daddies?

[JILLY *exits. The lights change.*]

SAM: My mother used to tell me that I needed a hobby like my Uncle John.

[LORRAINE *enters. She is* SAM'S *mother.*]

LORRAINE: Having too much time on one's hands is a dangerous thing.

SAM: But since Uncle John's flight, she doesn't say that anymore.

LORRAINE: There are all sorts of hobbies for a boy your age. Baseball card collecting. Stamp collecting. Butterfly collecting.

SAM: I wanna build a plane in our basement and fly it over the farm in North Dakota where Uncle John went down.

LORRAINE: I NEVER WANNA HEAR YOU SAY ANOTHER WORD ABOUT PLANES OR BASEMENTS OR MONTANA!

SAM: North Dakota.

LORRAINE: Whatever. It's sick! Do you wanna leave your family like your Uncle John did?

SAM: He didn't leave.

LORRAINE: Then what happened to him?

SAM: He had an accident.

LORRAINE: He senselessly wasted his life and left your cousin Jilly without a daddy and your Auntie Cheryl without a husband. He even left you without an Uncle John, didn't he?

SAM: He's still my Uncle John.

LORRAINE: In spirit, of course, he'll always be your Uncle. But wouldn't it have been nice if he could be here now. Don't you wish he hadn't built that plane and attempted that crazy flight to North Dakota.

SAM: Montana.

LORRAINE: Whatever. I bet your Uncle John wishes he could be here with you.

SAM: I bet he wished he had made it to Montana.

LORRAINE: The point is: Unlike your father, your Uncle John never learned to be a realist. A 295-pound man should have better sense than to squeeze into an ultra-light plane and fly it to Montana when he has a beautiful wife and child. When you have a wife and child of your own, you'll understand this.

SAM: If having a wife and child means not flying to North Dakota to see where Uncle John went down, then I'm never gonna have 'em.

LORRAINE: That's what you say now. But when you're a big boy you'll meet someone who'll make you feel differently.

SAM: Never. [*He pretends to fly his plane.*] Next stop Grassy Butte, North Dakota.

LORRAINE: I told you, Sam: No planes, no basements, and no North Dakota! If you don't stop it, I will take that away from you.
[LORRAINE *exits. The lights change. In the motion of landing his toy plane,* SAM *drops to the floor and begins to write a letter. As* SAM *speaks,* FARMER JOHN *enters.*]

SAM: Dear Mr. Farmer John:
Hello to you. My name is Sam. I am thirteen years old. My Uncle John crashed the plane that he built in my basement into your dairy farm in Grassy Butte, North Dakota. I'm writing to ask you the following questions in regards to my Uncle John. 1) How did you feel when you heard that the man whose plane dropped onto your farm had the same name as you? 2) Were any animals hurt in the crash? ...

FARMER JOHN: [*Continuing* SAM's *letter.*] 3) Do you have a son and if so how old is he? 4) Could I come and visit you this summer 5) Did you happen to find a good luck card that I made for my Uncle John and that I gave to him before his flight. I would like it for my Uncle John scrapbook.

I look forward to your answers. Please say hello to Mrs. Farmer John and any Farmer John children you might have — see question 3 ...

SAM: Sincerely, Sam, Uncle John's nephew and honorary co-pilot.

FARMER JOHN: Dear Sam:

It was very nice to hear from you. My family and I are so sorry about the tragic loss of your Uncle John. From all we've heard he was a remarkable man and a great, brave adventurer. Though we didn't know him, we think of him often, particularly during planting and harvest time when we're out in that corner of the field. Now called Uncle John's Field in your Uncle John's honor. In answer to your questions: 1) I hadn't really thought about it too much that his name's John and my name's John. But now that you mention it, it does make me feel like I know him a little better. 2) No, none of our animals were hurt in the crash. Even with the tremendous explosion, it was still quite far away from our farm buildings. I suppose a wild animal like a field mouse or rabbit might've been hurt, but I'm guessing that's not what you mean.

SAM: [*Continuing* FARMER JOHN'*s letter.*]..3) Yes, I do have a son. He's thirteen years old. I also have a daughter, age 15. 4) If it's okay with your mother and father, of course you can come out and visit. Just let us know. 5) No, no good luck card was recovered. As you may have heard that was a great deal of fire and it is highly unlikely that any paper would've survived such an inferno. However, one never knows and we'll keep looking. Again, let me say how sorry my whole family is about your loss. We pray that God delivers peace to him and all of you.

FARMER JOHN: Sincerely yours, Farmer John.

[*The lights change.* SAM *flies the toy yellow plane across the stage. It lands on a table that is made up for Thanksgiving. The table is below* UNCLE JOHN'*s plane.* SAM *parks the toy plane next to a large turkey sitting uncarved on the table.* LORRAINE, JILLY *and* CHERYL, UNCLE JOHN'*s widow, are seated around the table.*]

LORRAINE: Get that off the table, Sam.

SAM: It's a decoration.

LORRAINE: I said, get it off.

CHERYL: That's all right, Lor. I know Sam is just showing his love for his Uncle John.

LORRAINE: He shouldn't have toys on the table.

SAM: It's not a toy. It's a model.

LORRAINE: Whatever it is, get it off.

[SAM *pretends that the plane takes off from the table and he lands it under the chair that he sits on.*]

JILLY: Why aren't Sam and I sitting at the kid's table?

CHERYL: Because there's no kid's table this year.

JILLY: Why not?

CHERYL: Thanksgiving's just a little gathering this year. And besides, you always complain when you have to sit at the kid's table.

JILLY: I know, but this is lame; it's just like a regular dinner.

LORRAINE: It's not a regular dinner; it's special 'cos we're all together.

SAM: Not Uncle John.

CHERYL: In spirit, your Uncle John is with us. Just like in spirit your father is with us…

SAM: I got a letter yesterday from Farmer John and he said I could come visit this summer.

CHERYL: Who?

LORRAINE: Sam…

SAM: The dairy farmer in North Dakota.

LORRAINE: I forgot that his name was John.

SAM: They had the same name.

JILLY: So do a lot of people …

SAM: He said that I can come and visit him in North Dakota. He has a boy my age and also a daughter.

JILLY: Can I go?

SAM: No.

JILLY: Why not?

SAM: 'Cos I'm gonna build a plane and fly there and you called that crazy...

JILLY: My mom can drive me there ...

LORRAINE: Sam, Jilly, please. First of all: Sam is not going to North Dakota.

JILLY: See...Crazy, woo-woo...Just like my Daddy ...

CHERYL: Jilly...

SAM: I'm going...

LORRAINE: Sam, what did I tell you about that?

CHERYL: No, no, Lor, it's okay...I understand Sam's curiosity. The truth is, Sam, there's not much to see. It's just a corn field. And all this corn is so tall that I couldn't even see what little was left of the plane. Not that I wanted to.

LORRAINE: Why are we talking about this?

CHERYL: Really, it's okay. I can save Sam a trip. The funny thing is, there's not much difference between Sydney, Montana and Grassy Butte, North Dakota. John might just as well have tried to land in North Dakota instead of 70 miles further in Montana.

SAM: He didn't dream of North Dakota. He dreamed of Montana.

CHERYL: Well, he might as well have dreamed of North Dakota, because it was the same Goddamn dream. The same Goddamn corn fields. The same Goddamn road. The same Goddamn farm houses. I know because I drove from Montana to North Dakota with his dental records to identify what was left of his Goddamn body.

JILLY: Mommy swore...

LORRAINE: Enough! I don't wanna hear anymore about it! We're gonna carve the turkey and we're gonna talk about all the things we have to be thankful for.

[*There's quiet for a moment.*] Now who's gonna carve?

SAM: [*Quietly.*] I know they're not the same. Sydney and Grassy

Butte. Montana and North Dakota. I know it. 'Cos I have the same dream. Uncle John's dream.

[*The lights change.*]

UNCLE JOHN: [*Over the wind and plane noise.*] I'm not sure you can understand this, Sam, and I'm almost embarrassed to say it, but when I'm in this plane, the feeling is very sexual. There's not much room between me and the engine and it gives off the most remarkable vibrations. I once actually had a...a...very special feeling during the flight. The kind of feeling that I hope your father explained to you about while he was alive, and if not, that you'll find out about sooner or later in the school yard. It was right after take off. I don't think I was much out of Massachusetts. It didn't even have to do with sex. I felt so full of joy that I was flying towards my dream that it just took me by surprise. However, let me add, that in no way did this contribute to the crash. I was not having...such a feeling at the time the old Volkswagen engine began to make the first sounds of trouble.

[*Lights up on* SAM. *He is sitting on one of those children's rides of various shapes (usually horses or cars) that are frequently outside of convenience stores and "five and dimes" (in New York anyway) and that after a quarter is put in play music and move up and down in a rocking motion.* SAM *is on one shaped like an airplane. A red sign behind him says "Woolworth." and there are various signs announcing sale items. The ride ends.* SAM *puts another quarter in. The lights change. In the middle of the ride,* LORRAINE *enters with the* PRINCIPAL.]

LORRAINE: I know you don't want to tell me where you were, but why not tell, Principal Becker?

PRINCIPAL: We're concerned, Sam, not only because you've been missing school, but because you won't tell us where you've been. Now you know it's not safe to be wandering around by yourself.

SAM: It seems safe.

PRINCIPAL: It may seem safe, and certainly the Cape is for the most part, a nice safe place to grow up. But it's not safe by yourself, and not when we don't know where you were.

SAM: Is it safer than flying to Montana in a plane you built by yourself?

PRINCIPAL: Well, now that depends on where you were wandering...

LORRAINE: However, I think that Principal Becker would agree that each is stupid in its own way. It is stupid for a 295-pound man to fly an ultra-light plane to North Dakota...

SAM: Montana...

LORRAINE: Whatever. And it's stupid for a little boy to be out wandering in West Yarmouth when he's supposed to be in school.

PRINCIPAL: We don't like to say *stupid*...

LORRAINE: What do you like to say?

PRINCIPAL: Not smart.

LORRAINE: A 295-pound man flying in an ultra-light plane to Montana is *stupid*.

PRINCIPAL: But what Sam did is *not smart*.

LORRAINE: We don't know that because we don't know where he was.

PRINCIPAL: Now, Sam, why would a boy who gets high marks in school such as yourself be out wandering around away from the classroom?

SAM: I wasn't wandering.

PRINCIPAL: Then what were you doing?

SAM: I was practicing.

PRINCIPAL: Practicing what?

SAM: For my trip to North Dakota.

LORRAINE: You're not going to North Dakota.

SAM: I took her for some spins around the Cape to see how she feels.

UNCLE JOHN: [*Above the wind and the airplane noise.*] And Damn if she isn't soft, Sammie-boy.

SAM: Like a cloud with wings.

UNCLE JOHN: You'd think she was one of those big birds.

SAM: The new wings make all the difference.

UNCLE JOHN: And having all this weight is gonna be a blessing in disguise. I'm like a built in stabilizer.

SAM: I thought I'd have to stop maybe four or five times a day 'cos of the rough flyin', but now ...

UNCLE JOHN AND SAM: I think I'll be able to make it to Montana in two or three days.

[*As* SAM *and* UNCLE JOHN *complete the following,* SAM's *ride is coming to an end. The music and plane slow down.*]

PRINCIPAL: Now, Sam, everyone knows that an imagination is a good thing. Lord knows that we encourage it here at Kennedy School. But there is work time and play time. Now you must learn to be realistic and separate the two.

[*The lights change.*]

UNCLE JOHN: [*Over the wind and the plane sounds.*] I thought about your old man a lot during my flight. Boy did I love him, Sam. I wish he would've taken more of an interest in the plane, but, you know, that's not like him. Owning your own drugstore like that is a lot of work and he didn't have time to futz around with me. I'll tell you what though: I bet I would've gotten him up here. Oh, yes. I can picture it. You know what he once said to me, Sam. It was one of the few times I could get him down in the basement to work on the plane. He was having a great time, and he said that he would've liked to have been able to spend more time with us. He really did. And then he said, "I hope my son doesn't go into retail. I know a lot of fathers want their sons to follow in their footsteps, but I think Sam would be better off doing something else." That's not an easy thing for a father to say. But he always wanted what was best for you. Sometimes during my journey I imagined that your dad was flying with me. I'd point out to him all the incredible things that I was experiencing and it made the experience more vivid for me. Your dad was one of us, Sam, even though he didn't always show it. He had his head in the clouds, and don't let your mother tell you otherwise.

[*The lights change.* SAM *flies his toy yellow plane across the stage. He lands it in front of the newly replaced wall of his basement.* SAM *begins to feel the wall with his hands. Behind him is a bumper pool table which he doesn't notice.* LORRAINE *enters. She watches him for a few beats.* SAM *sits in front of the wall.*]

LORRAINE: The builder said that we would save an extra fifty dollars a month in heating costs now that our basement has four walls again.

SAM: How am I going to get my plane out?

LORRAINE: This isn't an airplane hanger; it's a basement.

SAM: It makes the basement look funny.

LORRAINE: No, it makes the basement look normal. When your Uncle John turned it into an airport, then it looked funny.

[SAM *continues to study the wall, as* LORRAINE *crosses to the bumper pool table.*]

　　Hey, did you see what I got you?

SAM: No.

LORRAINE: It's a bumper pool table.

[SAM *turns around.*]

SAM: A what?

LORRAINE: [*As she takes a shot.*] A bumper pool table.

SAM: Where am I going to put the wing assembly?

LORRAINE: I thought maybe you'd want to play with it until you got started on your plane. You know, you're becoming a big boy. You already had your Bar Mitzvah. You're gonna want a place you can play with your friends.

SAM: Bumper pool?

LORRAINE: Before he died, your dad dreamed of turning this basement into a rec room. He thought it'd be fun for you as you got older. He wanted to put in video games, and a TV, and a pool table. Things like that. Perhaps a place for both of you. But you know your father. He had a big heart. He couldn't say no to anyone. John wanted to move his plane in, and, of course, your father said yes.

SAM: His big heart just stopped.

LORRAINE: Yes, it did.

SAM: Like the Volkswagen engine.

LORRAINE: What?

SAM: That Uncle John had in the "Cheryl." Sometimes it'd just stop.

LORRAINE: C'mon, try it.

[*She takes another shot.*] It's fun.

[SAM *crosses over with the plane. He tries to land it on the felt. The plane hits one of the bumpers and flips over. As the lights change.*]

UNCLE JOHN: [*Over the wind and the plane noise.*] When I got to North Dakota, I really thought I was going to make it. I was actually comfortable for the first time during the journey. I was imagining what I would say to Cheryl when I saw her at the Sydney, Montana airport. You know, all sorts of funny comments. I had finally decided on one about no longer paying the premiums on that special life insurance she made me take out.

[*The lights change.* SAM *lands his plane at the feet of* JILLY, CHERYL *and* LORRAINE *who are all wearing black. It is* UNCLE JOHN'*s funeral. A* RABBI *is speaking.*]

RABBI: We may not know where he is, but like Jonah in the belly of the whale, he will not escape the sight of God. He was not Ulysses or Jason of Argonaut fame. He was a Jew. A man not destined for heroic and great adventures or wanderings. A good man. A mensch. A simple mensch on this earth who brought laughter to those who knew him, a quality product to those who bought his linoleum tiles, and love to his family and friends. Uncle John, though your body is lost, you are not lost in the sight of your God. As you are not lost in the eyes of your friends and family on this earth. Please recite with me.

THE RABBI *and* THE MOURNERS: Yis-ga-dol vi'yis-ka-dash sh'may ra-bo, B'ol-mo dee-v'ro chir-u-say, v'yam-leech mal-chu-say…

[*The lights change.*]

SAM: Everyone was so proud of Jilly because she didn't cry at the funeral. My mother said she was a strong little girl. I cried like a little baby. Be strong, my mother said. Your cousin Jilly is going to need you.

[*Lights up on* JILLY. *She wears her black dress.*]

JILLY: Watcha doin' in the basement?

SAM: I'm thinkin'.

JILLY: What about?

SAM: It looks funny without Uncle John's plane.

JILLY: I told you he was crazy.

SAM: It's not nice to say that about him after he's dead.

JILLY: He's my dad. Dead or not I can say anything I want about him, and I say he was crazy.

SAM: Shhh. My mother says he can hear us.

JILLY: So. He knows he's crazy. Look what happened to him. I bet all the way down he thought to himself: "I'm crazy. I'm crazy. I'm a crazy dad!"

[*Lights up on* UNCLE JOHN]

UNCLE JOHN: [*Over the wind and the airplane noise.*] I never felt so alive. Even after the old Volkswagen engine sputtered out completely, I didn't think, "Oh, this was a mistake, John. You shouldn't have done this." I thought, "Wow, I just really lived. I would like to live more like this. Unfortunately, I probably won't have the chance now." And then, of course, I thought, "Damn, I wish I had lost that twenty pounds so I had room for a parachute."

JILLY: [*She yells at the plane above the stage.*] Crazy, crazy, crazy dad!

SAM: You're crazy for yelling at a dead person.

JILLY: Your mother said that you have to be nice to me on account of my dad dying.

SAM: I'm trying.

JILLY: You want me to lift up my funeral dress and show you my underpants.

[SAM *looks at* JILLY *and then in the direction of where* UNCLE JOHN *was building the plane in the now empty basement. He then looks back at* JILLY.]

SAM: I guess so.

[JILLY *pulls up her funeral dress. The lights go out on* JILLY.]

SAM: When I'm old enough to go to Grassy Butte, North Dakota by myself, I will. I'll fly there in a plane that I make in this very basement. I'll find Farmer John's field and when I fly over it white plumes of smoke will shoot out the back of my plane and form the words "Uncle John Was Here" exclamation point. And after a low pass over the field where I will tip my wings to Farmer John and his family, I will make it that final 70 miles to Montana. I will make it for my Uncle John. Outta the big sky into big sky country.

UNCLE JOHN: [*Over the wind and the sounds of his engine sputtering, as he struggles to control his plane:*] Why Montana, Sam?

SAM: Because it's so magnificent.

UNCLE JOHN: [*Over the sounds of his engine sputtering even worse and the plane taking more effort to control.*] You know, it's 1994; they have roads that go to Montana. Or big jets.

SAM: I know, but it's not the same.

UNCLE JOHN *continues to try and control the plane and its sputtering engine. The engine emits a couple of last gasps and coughs. It then stops completely. The lights slowly fade on* UNCLE JOHN *and the plane as the sounds rise of the plane's erratic and sudden descent. There remains a soft spotlight on* UNCLE JOHN's *peaceful face and a dim light on* SAM *who is bringing his toy plane down for a safe landing. The sounds of* UNCLE JOHN's *fall fade out with the lights that were illuminating each of them. The sound of a crash is not heard.*

END OF PLAY

Madeleine George

THE MOST MASSIVE WOMAN WINS

Madeleine George

Madeleine George's plays, *Sweetbitter Baby* and *The Most Massive Woman Wins*, were produced in the 1993 and 1994 Young Playwrights Festivals at Playwrights Horizons and the Public Theater. Madeleine is a writing teacher and a story analyst, holds a degree in linguistics from Cornell University, and is a member of the Dramatists' Guild.

CHARACTERS

CARLY: 31 years old. In acid washed jeans, a rhinestone-studded denim jacket and a sweatshirt with high-top Reebok sneakers.

CEL: 29 years old. In a long dress. Her name is pronounced "Seel", it's short for Celia.

SABINE: 27 years old. In à la mode nineties officewear.

RENNIE: 17 years old. In overalls and a flannel shirt. She is a high school senior.

SCENE: *The play takes place in a liposuction clinic waiting room.*

TIME: *1990's.*

MUSIC: *Preshow music: "Dr. Feelgood," "The Weight." Playout: "Satisfaction," all by Aretha Franklin. Preshow music should be completely out by the time the house goes to half.*

GENERAL NOTES:

— All four women do not have to be overweight.
— Rennie is the only bulimic.
— It is important the play be established as humorous from the outset.
— A great deal of the 'dialogue' is directed out to the audience; they are often able to pick up on each others' thoughts without speaking straight at one another.
— The chants are genuine hopscotch, jumprope and handclap rymes from my own childhood and other children in Amherst, Massachusetts.
— We used blocking inspired by children's games: *London Bridge* and *Mulberry Bush* for the scoliosis check, *Red Rover* for the thesis defense, *Musical Chairs* for Carly's job interviews.

Monologue Notes

— Each monologue is delivered out to the audience.

— The three women not speaking at any one time should not look at the speaker, but in some way should be found to indicate that they are listening--stomps, thigh slaps, or claps that punctuate moments of tension or anger, for example. In the 'dance, run, jump, fly' sequence at the end of Cel's monologue the other three women did a slow flap of their arms, reprising the bird movement from earlier in the play. At that point they also turned to look at Cel.

— Carly talks hard and fast and never gets sentimental, but she loves her kid.

—Sabine is extremely hard on herself and never gives herself a break; instead of getting sad she always gets angry, right through to the very last line

—Rennie is perpetually panicked and jumpy; it's as if there's nothing holding her down to the floor. She laughs a lot to disguise her fear.

—Cel is not crazy. Her monologue is driven by her own need to tell her story. She does not relive the moment of her self-immolation, she tells us about it (this is important). Realization and catharsis come at the very end of the monologue, not before.

SETTING: *Waiting room of a liposuction clinic, furnished with four chairs.*

AT RISE: *The light is bright and sterile.* SABINE, CEL, CARLY *and* RENNIE *are seated on the chairs. For several minutes they stare at their magazines, fidget, cough, cross and recross their legs and flip magazine pages in an otherworldly, choreographed little dance.*

RENNIE: I'm about to have my body surgically removed.

CEL: [CEL'S *chant runs underneath the others' comments.*] Cinderella dressed in yella...

RENNIE: They're taking stuff out — big chunks, sloppy hunks.

CEL: Went to the ball to meet her fella...

SABINE: I'm here for the ass and inner thigh combo.

CEL: On the way her girdle busted...

CARLY: He said my butt and my gut is the parts he would pay for.

CEL: How many people were disgusted?

CARLY: Aw, shit, I hate waiting. If I'm gonna do this I just wanna do it, you know?

RENNIE: Scared?

CARLY: It's not that...

RENNIE: If you're here you're here because you want to be here.

ALL: On the way her girdle busted
       How many people were disgusted?

RENNIE: One —

SABINE: Two —

CEL: Three —

CARLY: Four —

ALL: [*Addressing the audience*] Five —

CARLY: The other night my boyfriend goes to me, he's spread eagle on the couch giving his gut some air watching Monday Night Football and during the commercial he goes, "We don't have steak anymore. How come is it we never have steak?" I'm about to say, "You want steak, buy steak. Take it out a your paycheck, if you want steak so bad," but then he says to me, like, right in the same breath he goes, "What am I saying? You're too fat for steak. Last thing you need is fatty red meat." Just like that, then he tips back his beer and the conversation's over.

SABINE: What did you say to him?

CARLY: I don't know, nothing. It's like I can't tell him off. Then later he leaves me this liposuction ad he clipped from the classifieds on my bedside table with a signed blank check. Is the guy subtle or what?

SABINE: Shit...

CARLY: You think it doesn't make me sick? What's the matter with me that I can't tell Frank Nowak where to stick it? I'm a weenie, that's what. A big fat wimp. How am I supposed to look my own kid in the face?

ALL: My boyfriend gave me peaches
My boyfriend gave me pears
My boyfriend gave me fifty cents
and kicked me down the stairs!

CARLY: C'ai play too?

RENNIE: She's too fat for jump rope.

CARLY: That feeling, you know it, it's the one you've been getting since you were six years old.

ALL: Miss Suzy had a baby
She named her Mary Lynn
She put her in the bathtub
Just to see if she could swim
She drank up all the water
She ate up all the soap
She tried to eat the bathtub
but it wouldn't go down her throat!

CARLY: It starts like a tidal wave under your feet and grows and grows until you forget your name and the people you love and all you know is you have to eat.

CEL: You think if you dared to open your mouth all of creation would get sucked right in.

SABINE: You think about eating alone in your bed, making love to a Twinkie, devouring it desperately, *HUNGRY* for it.

CARLY: You sneak out of bed, you don't think he hears you, you run down the stairs to where you hid the Sugar Smacks behind the TV, you're alone at last and you're eating great fistfuls, hand over hand. It tastes like everything you never had.

SABINE: It rises from a moan to a wail in your ears, it's pulsing through your body, it's chocolate you're hearing. It's the middle of the night and there's a winter storm warning, you're about to drive across town for a 52 ounce bar of Toblerone love.

RENNIE: Now you're gorging, cramming it thick down your throat, all Chewy Chips Ahoy and no room to breathe, you have to you have to you have to have it, then you're doubling over, spitting and shaking, face in the toilet, so sorry, so ashamed.

CARLY: You eat and you eat until you can't fit another bite into your body, you're bloated, drowned from the inside out.

SABINE: A beached whale, you can't move an inch.

CEL: You're done.

SABINE: You're done for.

RENNIE: So you throw out the evidence. Flush down the rest.

SABINE: Regain control.

CARLY: And you go back to doing what you were doing before.

[*They reprise the waiting dance.*]

SABINE: But you know you did it.

RENNIE: You may be making like everything is fine fine fine but you know what you've done, you bit it, you blew it.

CARLY: It's your fuckin fault — you lost control.

CEL: You know better than that.

SABINE: So it's time to make an adult decision.

CARLY: [*Smacks her own butt.*] Throw out the evidence.

RENNIE: You think of every sin in your past —

CEL: Every slice of pie —

CARLY: Every french fry —

SABINE: Every chocolate croissant —

RENNIE: You know it's all in there, simmering under your skin, and this nice man is gonna get rid of it all. Purify you.

ALL: Clean slate.

RENNIE: The ultimate purge.

SABINE: You are responsible for your own behaviour.

ALL: You are responsible.

RENNIE: You are guilty.

[*Lights shift, a whistle is blown.*]

CEL: [*Bellowing.*] Scoliosis check!

[CARLY, RENNIE *and* SABINE *scramble into position down center.*]

CEL: Shirts off!

CARLY: [*To* RENNIE.] She's such a fatso.

RENNIE: [*To* CARLY.] She weighs a hundred and four, I peeked at the scale.

CARLY: [*To* RENNIE.] Oh gross, look, she's getting boobs.

CEL: Bend at the waist!

CARLY: If you get them early it means you're a slut.

CEL: Rotate to face me!

RENNIE: I hope I don't get them.

CEL: Touch your hands to the floor!

CARLY: It's her fault cause she always eats two desserts at lunch.

CEL: Rotate again!

CARLY: We'll never get them like she's got them.

CEL: Stand up!

RENNIE: We'll never be so disgusting as her.

[*Lights shift, a whistle is blown.*]

SABINE: Look who's not playing.

CEL: [*Sassy.*] She's excused.

CARLY: She's always excused. Bitch.

CEL: She can't play dodgeball, she's ginormous!

SABINE: Gigundo!

CARLY: Gigantoid!

CEL: [*Yelling to* RENNIE.] Hey fatso, what position are YOU playing, huh?

RENNIE: [*Quietly.*] Offense. [*Lights shift, a whistle is blown, they scramble into a new formation.*]

SABINE: [*Announcing.*] In defense of my thesis: "Images of Women in Cold War and Post-Cold War Era Media Colon Self-Denial and Self-Esteem." [*Confidently.*] I refer you once again to both Kruger and Wolf as well as to Baudrillard's discussion of the hypnotizing image.

[*She takes a deep breath, then speaks quickly.*]

In conclusion I would like to emphasize my belief that this and related subject matters are pertinent, if not crucial, to our postmodern society. Although inquiry into such subjects is somewhat scarce in journals today, I predict that as the information age hits its stride, and as feminist thought becomes more seamlessly integrated into mainstream American consciousness, we will see a proliferation of influential and powerful work concerning the subjugation of women's bodies through media images. Thank you.

RENNIE: Ms. Rowe. Can you explain again ex-act-ly how this subject is relevant? I can't see how this topic merits scholarly investigation when it has such a minute effect on the population as a whole.

SABINE: If eating disorders are as prevalent among women as recent studies show, and if women comprise as they do 52% of the population I think you'll find this is quite a relevant subject for investigation —

CEL: [*Cutting in.*] I fail to understand why these women can't simply "get over" disorders that you claim are caused by looking at two-dimensional images.

SABINE: Obviously it's a bit more complicated than that —

CARLY: [*Cutting in.*] As every person is responsible for his own attitudes about himself, it should be a simple matter for a person to alter his image of self, should it not?

SABINE: [*Stumbling over words.*] Once again I'd like to remind you that studies show physical appearance, that is, conformity to societally-established standards of beauty, has a much greater impact on women's lives than on men's, this includes social status, marital status, income and work-related achievements —

RENNIE: [*Cutting in.*] It seems to me you're getting a little emotional about this. I can understand why this hits a little close to home for you. For that reason I would have advised you to choose a topic you could remain somewhat objective about.

[*Lights shift, whistle.*]

CARLY: What about benefits?

RENNIE: [*Strongly emphasizing the 'Mizz.'*] We haven't yet decided if this is an appropriate job for you, Ms. —

CARLY: Kinski.

RENNIE: Let's hold off our discussion of fine points and sundries until we are able to come to a full understanding.

CARLY: Sure thing, sir. [*Whistle.*]

SABINE: Let me be frank, Ms. —

CARLY: Kinski.

SABINE: I don't think you have fully considered the physical taxation that is put on a person in this line of work.

CARLY: Sir, I been in food service all my life.

SABINE: The waitstaff here are part of our family. And because of the extreme demands placed on their persons I demand that every member of the family be in peak physical condition.

CARLY: Alls I'm saying sir is I can do this job and I just wanna know about the benefits you — [*Whistle*]

CEL: [*Overlapping.*] I'm afraid I'm not fully getting through to you, Ms. —

CARLY: Kinski, Kinski.

CEL: Allow me to speak as plainly as possible. I really don't think the restaurant can use a woman of your stature at this time. Please don't take this personally, but with the aesthetic atmosphere I am trying to cultivate there are certain, hmmm, discrepancies that cannot be tolerated.

CARLY: I been trying to tell you —

[*Whistle.*]

RENNIE: [*Cutting in.*] Most of the girls I hire are eighteen, nineteen years old. [*Whistle.*]

SABINE: They haven't been through what you've been through I'm sure. [*Whistle.*]

CEL: I hope you won't be unduly upset by this. [*Whistle.*]

RENNIE: Not everything can be fair in this world, I'm afraid.

[*Lights shift, whistle is blown. During* CEL'S *trial,* SABINE *paces the perimeter of the stage calling off.* RENNIE *and* CARLY *become* CEL'S *reflected image in the mirror.*]

CEL: My husband has a theory. He's figured it out.

SABINE: Cel!

CEL: My husband says to me Cel, can't you see yourself in the mirror? I say Yeah.

SABINE: Cel!

CEL: He says so why don't you do something about it, it's for your own good he says. You know about the heart failure and the brain tumors and amputations, but how many times I have to tell you what really happens to girls who get too big —

SABINE: Celia!

CEL: [*Bitter, completing the quote.*] — honey.

SABINE: [*Calling for her.*] Honey?

CEL: He says fat girls go crazy more than thin girls do.

SABINE: Goddamn it girl, where did you get to now?

CEL: It has to do with metabolism, he says, he read it in the encyclopedia, because fat girls let their cells get unbalanced.

SABINE: Ce-lie, it's freezing in here!

CEL: See your body has to send more blood down to the fat so it can't spend the time that it should in your brain. It's like there's this system inside you and everything in it has to balance, if you add a little too much of one thing you throw off the rest.

[*The mirror reflections begin to flap their arms like birds, then turn away from* CEL, *released.*]

SABINE: For Christ's sake, Cel, what is going on here in the middle of November? Every window and door is swung out on its hinges, the place is a mess, there are birds flying by me in the goddamn kitchen, what's the matter with you, girl? What is wrong with you, woman?

CEL: [*Still to the audience.*] That's why he said maybe a surgical cure, so I can get rid of that parasite fat. I can maybe start acting more normal he says.

[*Lights shift, final whistle is blown.*]

ALL: Little Baby Sally was sick in bed
    Sally called for mama and her mama said
    Little Baby Sally you're not sick
    All you need is a peppermint stick.

[*Lights shift, hospital gowns fly in, the women stand behind them and undress during the next exchange, then put the gowns on.*]

CARLY: My mama was — she used to say "plump and juicy."

RENNIE: My mother said for big girls like me it was ugly to let people see the stuff you were made of. Especially legs and shoulders and the inside of your mouth.

SABINE: Our mothers all taught us the same thing.

CARLY: Hush up, Carly girl.

SABINE: Sit still till we get to grandma's and mama'll give you a cookie.

CEL: If you're good you can lick the bowl.

CARLY: Do you kiss your mother with that mouth?

RENNIE: Sit up straight and eat only what you're offered.

SABINE: Children are starving in Denmark.

CEL: Eat your peas.

SABINE: Or was it Detroit?

CARLY: Open wide!

RENNIE: What's the matter, don't you feel well?

CARLY: What's wrong, don't you want dessert?

SABINE: Here, darling, have some of mama's homebaked cherry pie.

CEL: Chicken-fried steak.

RENNIE: Chocolate mousse. [*They all laugh and "mmm" in agreement.*]

CARLY: Baby, you are so be-yoo-tiful, just like a calendar girl with those big brown eyes and that beautiful skin!

RENNIE: Why did everyone always tell me I had beautiful skin?

CARLY: And babes, someday you'll thank me for letting you put on that extra padding. When your airplane crashes on the highest peak of the Himalayas all those skinny passengers are gonna starve to death seven ways till Sunday and you will survive for months and months, living only off what you have stored in your tush.

SABINE: Mama's always right. You just wait.

[RENNIE, CEL *and* SABINE *return to their corners to sit, lights up on* CARLY *in the center.*]

CARLY: No my mama was not always right. No, you shoulda seen her when he'd come home nights, the whole place'd get quiet like the grave, I swear, she'd be pussyfootin' around him jumping like a sick kitten every time he made a move…all you could hear was him chewing with his mouth open and his silverware hitting the plastic plate.

It's too late for my mama, it's too late for me now. But the day my kid was born I made it a promise that she was gonna know who she was. No one was gonna walk all over my kid. No one was gonna give her a goddamned blank check.

Then the other day I come home from work and there she is, my stupid kid, sitting on the bathroom floor, leaning against the tub, and her long blonde hair is dyed pitch black, I swear, black as tar, and it's dripping black rivers all down her face and her neck… I could have killed her right then and there, I wanted to knock her head off of her skinny little neck.

Instead of killing her I say, Jesus Christ, what the hell did you do to your hair, and she's crying and choking and she goes, Ma! and points at the counter. I looked and I swear I thought I was going to toss my cookies. She has got one of these EPT plus pregnancy tests laid out there, you know, the little stick kind? Pink, pregnant, white, not pregnant...there's that little stick leaning up against the box it came in and the end is as bright pink as an Easter egg, pink as all fuck, pardon my French, pink like a baby's butt is pink. Talk about history repeating itself. Suddenly I'm sixteen again with that sinking feeling in my stomach looking at the little test tube, holding it up against the light bulb in the upstairs closet....

So I'm trying to figure out what exactly the black hair has got to do with the pink stick. I say, Is that or is that not an EPT plus pregnancy test? and she nods, so I say, Is that or is that not a pink stick you got there? and she says, It's pink. I say, So you're pregnant, so you dyed your hair black? She starts sobbing and wailing and she goes, I knew you wouldn't understand, you never understand anything about me! She bangs past me and stomps down the hall and slams the bedroom door behind her. I'm thinking, what's to understand? You're totally nuts!

I'm standing there alone in the bathroom. The place looks like a tornado hit, there's little bottles and vials and tubes all over, with that little pink baby-positive stick lying right in the middle like the eye of the hurricane, the evil eye, more like, still and pink and sticking its tongue out at me. Ha. You lost. You fucked up. I'm thinking, what happened? I thought only fat girls didn't know what they were doing. My kid's a beauty, gorgeous, skinny, tall, why the hell didn't she stand up for herself? How could she let this happen? She's got no goddam spine!

Then I'm back to the time when she was just two years old, the first time I saw her throw a tantrum. It was in the kitchen, over a purple popsicle. I was so surprised at the force inside her little body. She stamped her bare feet on the kitchen floor and balled up her fists and bared her tiny white teeth at me, and when I said, No, and shut the refrigerator door with the toe of my shoe she looked up into my face and squinted, she wasn't three feet tall, and her mouth got tiny like the...head of a nail, and I knew I had someone to contend with then.

So I go into the bedroom, sit down on the edge of the bed and pat her on the back. Stacey, sweets, hey, hey, it's alright. You gotta be strong and make your own choice, but whatever decision you want to make, I'm behind you, okay? We'll do whatever you choose. She stops sniffing. She breathes in and out. I say, So, listen, uh...have you talked to the guy about this yet? And she says, nasty, No, Ma, God. Boys don't like girls who boss them around.

[*Lights down on* CARLY, *up on* SABINE *in her corner, during the course of the monologue she moves center.*]

SABINE: Like my friend Michael. Michael and I, we are best friends. We go for sushi and foxtrot once a month at the full moon. The thing is, all our conversations go like this: Michael tells me about his love life, I support him. Michael whines about his girlfriend, I console him. Michael moans about the horrors of latex, I sympathize, I hug him, I make him tea, and recently I have found myself possessed with rage absolutely every time I lay eyes on him. Because I am so very tired of being everyone's warm and fuzzy sounding board. I want to be a full-blown sexual threat right now. I want to get down on my hands and knees and do it, sweaty, hot, savage, wrong, morally rep-re-hensible...If my mother could hear me now... she wasn't out of her foundation garments long enough to have sex. I was an immaculate conception. My father stuck his tongue in her ear and bang, there I was, I appeared just like that on the kitchen counter in an attractive presentation basket. That's how we fat women do it, you know. We just close our eyes and think beautiful thoughts and our offspring arrive with the afternoon mail.

In undergrad psychology we learned about these people, they were called split-brain patients, and each hemisphere of their brain could work on a task without the other half knowing. In the films they showed us they taught this one guy to build blocks into towers with his left hand only. Then separately they taught his right hand to tear block towers down. On the last day of the experiment they let both the hands work together — the guy actually fought with himself in this film — his left hand tried to build a tower while his right hand constantly wrecked whatever he made. The hands started slapping each other and wrestling with the same block...

The one half of me, see, won't take no for an answer. This me's gonna go out there and take the corporate world by storm, if that's what I decide I want to do, or climb mountains, or pump gas, or write for TV, or...become a stock broker if I happen to feel like it. I do not need male approval to achieve my life goals. Like a fish needs a bicycle, and so on and so on.

But I just can't ignore my pathetic other side — it's so whiny and "needy" inside of me. I yearn for...human touch, God, it's embarrassing, sometimes all I want is to be looked at, admired, soothed and caressed. I still want the power, I still want to make money and go mountaineering. But the thing I want most right now, God, Santa, Gloria Steinem, is some person to love me and sleep in my bed.

First I hate myself for it, then I forgive myself lovingly, then I yell at myself for going soft on myself. Then I cry, usually, and then I get sullen and scowl. Stomp around the place dropping dishes and breaking bric-a-brac. Backlash! I scream, backlash, Sabine! You're contributing to the undeclared war against women! How could you! How dare you! You ought to be shot! Then I usually have a marshmallow sundae to calm myself down.

The saddest thing is, I've got no one to blame. God damn, I wrote my dissertation on this, I know the eight key symptoms and the ten warning signs and the twelve-step recovery program like the back of my hand. How can I be so smart and so stupid?

So I've made a very adult decision. If I can't change the world, I have to change myself. I'm gonna lay on my back and suck up the gas and fall into a deep sleep, and when the prince kisses me I'm gonna wake up and be beautiful. And then I'm gonna flush all my feminist morals down the can and I'm gonna sashay my butt out into the glittering suburban night and I'm gonna get laid, goddamnit. Like my mom used to say — you've made your cake, now you have to eat it. I hear you, Ma. Ain't it the truth.

ALL: [*Quietly.*]

> This is the way we bake our cake
> bake our cake
> bake our cake.
> This is the way we bake our cake.
> So early Friday morning.

[*A flashbulb pops and* RENNIE *is propelled into center.*]

RENNIE: The first picture of me is at my first birthday party. In this one I am screaming with laughter and holding my hands up to show the camera that I am covered with chocolate cake. My face is smeared with it, it is all over the front of my pretty pink dress. Apparently I was quite verbally advanced, and my parents were showing me off when my uncle Jake said, Oh yeah? How smart is she? She's a genius, says my mother, she understands everything. Try it. She'll do anything you say.

So…Rennie, says my uncle Jake, smush that chocolate cake all over your face, sweetheart. Will you do that for me?

And I did it of course because I was just that smart and I ruined my dress and they took a picture of me humiliating myself when I was twelve months old.

[*Flashbulb pops.*]

This one is my mother's favorite. It's of her and me on one of our mother-daughter days, we're on the steps of the Met looking very close and what you don't see is Mother boring her knuckles into the small of my back saying Straighten up, sweetheart, it lengthens your neck. Now glow, come on, glow. We want this one to glow.

For awhile there is an absence of photos — when tummies are no longer little-girl cute. Mother hides me at family gatherings and I seem always to end up behind pieces of furniture. So we have no extant record of the long years of wanting, of wanting and wanting and being denied. Reaching for bread and peanut butter and having Slimfast thrust into my twelve-year-old fist. Mother says No, I am putting my foot down. She is putting her foot down, I see, and I see that to want and demand things is bad.

And when I finally want nothing, nothing at all, when I finally want so little I can barely get up in the morning, my head feels like a ten ton brick on my shoulders, my knees buckle walking from class to class, when I want so little the gentlest sounds scrape my ears and my skin is sore and my hair falls out, finally my mother pulls me out from behind the chaise longue-

and says This is my daughter Rennie! This is my wonderful, beautiful daughter. Out comes the camera!

[*Flashbulb pops.*]

The pictures reappear. All the while Mother says Sweetheart, you're beautiful. You really do glow.

[*Flashbulb pops.*]

In this one I am standing outside my own house, in a hideous dress I do not recall choosing, it is blue and it feels like a garbage bag next to my skin. I am wearing a floppy white orchid on my wrist and man, am I glowing. I am really fucking glowing. My smile is about this wide on my face though I don't know what I am smiling about because Andrew Marino has his hand on my back. We haven't even left the house yet, my mother is still snapping pictures and there he is, slinking his hand up my dress. Later we are in the dark and he is breathing so hard he is fogging the windshield and I say to him Andrew. No. No. And he says to me Rennie, you're beautiful. Please Rennie please, will you do it for me? I am saying, No, I am saying, Stop, but he does not hear me, I am not loud enough. I am so — weak. I am just...too...weak.

[*Flashbulb pops.*]

In this one my mother is getting remarried. She is a vision in indigo organdy, she looks half her age, her husband's in real estate. But heavens, where's Rennie? Rennie's not in this one. Rennie is wearing an attractive off-white linen pants suit, but she is not in her place at her mother's side because she is in the parish hall kitchen, devouring the three-foot-tall wedding cake meant to serve one hundred and eighty guests. It was just so pristine, floating there, with no one to guard it, no one to witness...I ate and I ate and I ate it all up until there wasn't one crumb left, not a single frosted rosette, and I held that whole cake inside my body, I had it all to myself. And then I threw it all up on the kitchen floor and I walked out the back door into the night.

[RENNIE *runs back to her chair, lights shift.*]

CARLY: I wonder what it'll actually be like.

SABINE: I've researched the procedure, I'll describe it if you want.

CARLY: Thanks but no thanks.

SABINE: You'll be knocked out, you won't feel a thing.

RENNIE: What are you afraid of? It's what we've been waiting for.

[*Lights shift, up on* CEL *in her corner. During the course of the monologue she moves up center and then progressively further downstage.*]

CEL: It starts with a girl maybe six maybe seven, looking down at herself seeing how — horrible she was! How gross like a monster. She didn't look anything like the other kids from 4-H, they were all skinny as rats from dragging goats through the mud and bending over fields in the blazing hot sun. In summer all kids' legs were scabby — but nobody had marks on them like I did, like Cel, Cel had some scars.

The first one came when I was six. I had split open my knee climbing through barbed wire and mama drove me to the hospital to get the thing stitched up with ugly dark thread, that's how deep it was. But I took those stitches out with scissors when I got home. I told my mama they came out in the bath but I could tell by the way she looked at me sidewise frying the eggs that she didn't believe it. All that summer I worked on my knee and by the time Labor Day rolled around my leg looked like it had been caught in a thresher, maybe.

After that she just seemed to find them, Cel, these cuts in her skin, these holes. They seemed to pop up without her even noticing. Some she put in there herself with the kitchen knives for killing the chickens or shears for the garden or the awl daddy used for punching holes in saddles.

Mama didn't know what to do with her girl. At first she didn't say anything, just folded her arms like so across her chest. What's happened to the backs of your feet she asked. You're picking those cuts of yours apart aren't you? What are you doing to yourself Celie? Why do you want to do such a thing to yourself? So she started buying extra boxes of bandaids and leaving them about the house in places she thought I might be likely to come across them. But I wanted to — take myself completely apart. I had dreams of my body parts spread out in the yard for everyone even the neighbors to see.

All the way through high school I did it at night when no one was looking. After my shower, when the skin was still soft. It was my thing to know. Then one day my husband found me on the floor of the bathroom, busted in without knocking...After that he kept watching me, keeping track where I went. I tried to lay still. I forgot things...left them to burn on the stove. My husband paced around and slammed the door on his way out. He accused me of letting the heat out in winter, letting animals in, stray cats and birds.

So I needed a final solution. Get rid of all of the flesh at once. I was poking a roaster chicken full of cloves getting ready for Sunday dinner and I went to light the broiler with a hard wooden match. Then it came to me. My body — I wanted to light it on fire. Hear the fat sizzle into smoke. With all the fat gone I could dance — more than that, I could run and jump and fly maybe even, just me and my bones running naked through the meadows feeling the breeze. It seemed so obvious — why hadn't I thought of this before? I struck one of the matches, stroked it smooth across the rough edge of the box and I could feel the flame sparking and growing and swallowing the match head. I held it in front of my face. It flickered in my own breath. My thighs would go up first I thought then the rest of me would catch on quick. I lifted my leg and dropped the match onto my pants. For a moment—nothing, then — warm hot my leg started to jump — my skin was on fire. I screamed without meaning to Oh my God. I reeled around to face the counter my hands out in front of me reaching — desperate — something — anything. Towel potholder glass of water...In my mind I heard Miss Moser from in front of the black board — stop, drop and roll, she said, if you ever catch fire just stop, drop and...

Later I went to the phone to call 911, shivering, numb. I

caught fire, I said calmly into the phone. I was cooking a chicken. It escaped.

[RENNIE, SABINE *and* CARLY *come over to* CEL *and touch her one by one. They all look at each other, then, embarrassed, start to return to their chairs.* CARLY *stops them by beginning the candy store chant.* SABINE *joins in, then* RENNIE, *so it sounds like a round. When they hit the "Doctor doctor will I die" line they each continue to chant that until they all say it together, including* CEL]

ALL: I met my boyfriend at the candystore
He bought me ice cream
He bought me cake
He brought me home with a belly ache
Mama mama I feel sick
Call the doctor quick quick quick

Doctor doctor will I die?

CARLY: Count to five and you'll survive.

RENNIE: One.

SABINE: Two.

CEL: Three.

CARLY: Four.

ALL: Five.

[*They look at each other, then simultaneously take off their gowns and drop them on the floor. In their underwear, they walk together downstage and stand facing the audience. The last few lines are light and full of relief.*]

CARLY: Once upon a time there was a very beautiful woman who hardly ever wanted or asked for anything until one day when she suddenly got — very extremely hungry.

CEL: So she said to her husband, honey, climb over that wall and get me some of them radishes I see growing down there in that garden.

SABINE: But this was no ordinary garden.

CARLY: This was no ordinary woman.

RENNIE: This was no ordinary hunger.

[*Two beats, lights bump out. End of play.*]

Stephen Hunt

THE WHITE GUY

Stephen Hunt

Stephen Hunt's one man show, *The White Guy*, premiered at the Public Theatre in New York in 1995. It has subsequently been produced in New York at Naked Angels (excerpts), at the HBO Workspace in Los Angeles, the Vancouver Men's Festival and the Winnipeg Fringe Festival.

His comedy, *Eye Spy*, was produced at the Soho Rep in 1994, directed by Wendy Fried and starring Terumi Matthews and Craig Carlisle. His black comedy *The Locomotion Man* was read at Ensemble Studio Theater's *Octoberfest '97*.

His comedies, *The Golfer, Insomnia, Stupid Sadists, Catherine* and *Sweeps Week* have been produced in New York at Off-Off Broadway theaters including La Mama, The West Bank Cafe, Naked Angels, Ensemble Studio Theatre and the Public Theatre.

A finalist in the 1997 Warner Brother's Comedy Writers Workshop, Stephen has written for stage, the page, film, TV and radio, from comedy to commentary to copywriter for ESPN. Currently, he's been commissioned to write a comedy pilot for Britain's Pearson TV. He was commissioned and developed an original comedy pilot for the Canadian Broadcasting Corporation (CBC) called *Danny's All-Star Joint*. Recently, his monologue Stromboli was filmed by the actress/director Karyn Parsons, starring Terumi Matthews.

A memoir of the short story writer Raymond Carver written by Stephen was published in *Remembering Ray: A Composite Biography Of Raymond Carver (Capra Press, 1993)* He has also written for a number of magazines and newspapers, including *Details, Saturday Night, The Toronto Globe and Mail, Winnepeg Free Press* and *Santa Monica City Scene*.

Stephen has an MFA from the University of British Columbia. He worked as a volunteer teaching playwriting at the 52nd Street Project in New York, and is a member of the Ensemble Studio Theatre. He lives in Santa Monica with his wife, the actress Melanee Murray-Hunt.

[*RISE on* THE WHITE GUY, *alone at center stage.*]

OK, I'm a white guy. I know it. It's obvious, right?
You probably think I'm this
domestic beer drinking,
red meat eating, *USA Today* reading,
ESPN watching,
normal, perfect home-owning
kinda guy!
And you'd be suprised,
how long I went
before noticing that I'm actually this
Bass Ale drinking,
sushi eating,
khaki-shorts wearing,
Bravo-Channel watching,
New Yorker reading
emotionally-arrested
kind of *renter!*
    [*Beat.*]
But then again,
To everybody else, lookin' back at me,
it's so obvious, I'm just one thing:
a white guy!
I'm part of a *tribe!*

Know what that means, don't you?

Construction workers sittin' on their high beams
when I walk by don't shout '*nice tits*'.
Women seeing me come towards them on the street
don't clutch their purses *tighter.*
    [*Beat.*]
Cops don't shoot me by accident.
Never.
Does not happen.

To live the life of a white guy,
in a white guy's world, well, it's, it's —

It's nice.
It's tremendous.

But frankly, it's not the greatest time to be me.
For one thing, my media role models suck.
The only thing you ever read about white guys these days
is either how mean we are or how mad we are.
Witness the collected films of Michael Douglas.
And one reason why so many of us are mad
is this certain intellectual perspective
held by universities and certain political parties and non-profit
theater across America — those season tickets theaters,
you know the ones I'm talking about, theaters
dedicated to serving audiences *smarter than usual*.
It's not something they say out loud — because a lot of us are
season ticket holders — but it's there, in the subtext,
of almost everything.

You just gotta listen for it.

It goes a little like this:
who invented patriarchy?
A white guy, livin' in a cave, tired of chasing down takeout.

Who invented Apartheid?
A white guy, who showed up one day in darkest Africa and said,
to hell with Holland, I'm stayin!
And I gotta be in charge!

Who ruined the Ozone Layer?
Well, let's just say — a white guy, with perfect hair,
driving his Ford Explorer 10 MILES A FRIGGING HOUR
down the Santa Monica Freeway!

Who stole rock and roll?
A fat, spangled jumpsuit wearin', 14 year old marryin', pill
devourin',
B-movie makin', Live-in-Hawaii,
Hunka-hunka burnin white guy!

Dead, on a stamp!
Looks we're the problem with everything!
But
To tell you the truth, when I was in college,
I hated white guys too!

In fact, I hated white guys so much —
I forgot I was one.
As much as I could.
I mean, let's face it — it's tough, when you recognize the enemy
— and it's you.
I had a limited set of choices to work with.
I couldn't become a non-white guy.
I was still attracted to women.
I was ashamed of my lifelong passion for competitive sports.
    [*Beat.*]
I became a lesbian!
    [*Beat.*]
I moved to Vancouver — a known lesbian haven.
What the hell.
I wanted to meet someone cute.
I had good lesbian hair, in those days.
    [*Beat.*]
I was not taken too seriously.
Those Western Canadian women seemed to sense right from the
    get-go
that I was a dilettante.
    [*Beat.*]
I hate that!
    [*Beat.*] [*Then, sadly:*]
I turned inward.
Started writing. Poetry. Bad, sad, shitty poetry.
Until I was completely disgusted with myself.
Then, I wrote a TV script — spec script — about a group of
    tough, yet sensitive lesbians.
Single moms by day, Canadian documentary filmmakers by night.
Called it…*Goddesses.*
I even sold it, to Canadian television.
You never know, with those wacky Canadians.

They called me in for a meeting one day.
Guy in charge, Phillip, he's about seventy, alcoholic,
his clothes don't match, he's got food bits stuck in his beard,
leans across his desk really slowly and says,
what's with all these LESBIANS?
     [Beat.]
Watch it, Phil, I said. You're *talking to one.*

The show never got made.

But now, looking back on my lost lesbian years, I feel OK.
It takes a while to figure out who you are.
You gotta go through stuff, experience life, and one day,
you wake up and you recognize yourself, and you say,
you nitwit! You're not a lesbian!
What the fuck were you thinking?
You're a white guy — and that's OK.

And to those of you out there who aren't white guys —
and I can feel you out there —
 — and you're welcome here —
you might think our little 5000 year winning streak came at your
expense.
You have a point there.
To you, I say, sorry about that.

And to those of you like me,
white guys who feel a little down,
a little browbeaten, a little frustrated, remember:
there are still things we can be proud of:

Who was first on the moon?
A white guy, with a five iron!

Who's almost all of the coaches?
White guys, even though they're almost none of the players.

Who's on the money?
White guys, white guys, and more white guys—and pyramids.

Who wrote *Death of a Salesman*?
A red white guy, a well-liked white guy.

Who were the Beatles?
Tell me a white guy is the problem with everything,
and I say, OK, we did steal rock and roll.
Guilty.
And we do make easy targets.
Don't shoot!

BLACKOUT

DETROIT

I long to go to Detroit, not Flint.
It is 1968 and I live in Manitoba, Canada.
And as I am seven, my world is divided in two:
places that are on television, and places that aren't.
Detroit is on television.
Flint isn't.
Flint has shopping, but shitty shopping.
Detroit has the Tigers.
I see the Tigers on TV all the time.
Ty Cobb played for the Tigers, in the twenties.
I read a book about Ty Cobb once.
Ty Cobb had a .367 lifetime average.
Do you know how high that is?

Dad, we could go to a game! It would be fun!
It's an American city!
Dad says, *No.*
    [*Beat.*]
Why not, Pop? We go through Flint every summer.
Flint sucks.

Why can't we go to Detroit?

Dad goes, We take one wrong turn at Detroit,
the blacks will turn over the trailer and set fire to it.
     [*Beat.*]
That was a suprise answer.

I don't know what to say.
I don't know any blacks.
There are no blacks where I come from.
The only thing I know about blacks are what I've read
in sports biographies — *From Ghetto to Glory, The Bob Gibson
     Story.*
Wilt Chamberlain, the only player to score 100 points in a game.
Willie Mays, the most exciting ballplayer of his era.
Willie Mays sounds so cool, he's my favorite player,
even though his era was never my era.

It's best not to argue with Dad, though.
Travelling is all business with him.
We go through Michigan on our way to Ontario
because gas is cheaper than in Canada.
We write down the mileage in a book, so we can figure out
miles-per-gallon. We keep track of what we spend.
We rise at dawn, to maximize daylight driving.
We always tell Customs the truth.

For me though, travelling isn't business at all.
It's total bonus points.

I'm thinking,
if the blacks realize we're from Canada,
they won't turn our trailer over and set fire to it!

Just point to the license plate, Pop!
We never did anything!
It's 1968, and they're burning down inner cities
across America, and just because Willie Mays is
your favorite ballplayer don't mean shit.

To nobody.

We skip Detroit.
I'm the Boss, Dad says, And you do what the Boss says.
When you're the Boss, you can go to Detroit.
Detroit's not going anywhere.

We pull up outside a shopping mall in Flint.
Who wants ice cream? Pop asks.
I'm buying — as if he doesn't buy everything.
My Dad gets out, then sticks his head back inside.
You coming in, or you just gonna sit there and sulk?
I don't speak. I'm never speaking again.
Have it your way, he says. We'll be inside if you change your
    mind.
They all go into the mall. I watch them, thinking, why is the right
    answer
always 'no' with him?
Sometimes, I think the guy got his degree from the University of
'No.'
That's when I make a promise to myself.
Someday, I'm getting out of there.
I'm gonna get to a place where people say 'yes.'
I'm goin' to Detroit.

[*Lights shift. Hat off.*]

MABUTI

Mabuti comes from Lesotho, a township by South Africa.
I can't picture this Lesotho place in my mind.
They don't have any teams from Lesotho.
They never get on television.
Lesotho is like, the Flint of South Africa.

Down there by South Africa, somewhere.

Country full of protestors, from the sounds of it.
Protesting what?
Well — South Africa. Apartheid. White Guys!
Who sound like the very worst white guys ever invented.
White guys even a white guy could hate.

Mabuti is a small man. He has a beard. He seems wise,
someone who puts the big picture before himself.
He has a bullet scar on his forehead.
That's where he got grazed.
That's what they call it when the bullet doesn't stick,
it just skims past you, leaving a permanent scar.
Mabuti has friends who weren't so lucky.
Mabuti came to Winnipeg. He goes to my university.
He is the first black man I know.

I meet him one day at a party at the university President's house.
Our university is sponsoring him.
Every year, we sponsor one person from someplace awful.
Generally ends up being a black guy, from Africa, as a rule.
We have Johannes Selassi, from Ethiopia.
Yohannes isn't what you think when you hear 'Ethiopia.'
He's not starving at all.
Yohannes claims he's related to the Emperor Halle Selassie,
and since none of us knows fuck all about Ethiopia, and hey —
they have the same last name —
we accept this as fact.

We got Grace Edward Galabuzzi, from Uganda.
Grace is a soccer player with astonishing posture.
Like Prince Charles.
And to tell you the truth, Grace seems more British than African.
But Mabuti is different. He seems truly African.
Mabuti is a wise jester, a prankster.
If Grace Edward Galabuzzi is an Empire man, Mabuti is his Irish
    counterpart.
Mabuti will always join ya for a drink.
And sometimes,
when he is drunk enough,

Mabuti hints at the horrors he has witnessed in life,
but he never goes into very much detail.
Of course, I do the right thing.
I'm always horrified by his stories — as if I could be anything but.
Mabuti makes me feel like he understands me.
In fact — and this is what's so great about the guy — he makes me
  feel
as if he understands how hard it is to be me,
listening to all those bad things that happened to him.

In summer, I lose track of the Africans.
They vanish from my life.
Whoosh! Africans, away.
I rediscover my old life, my high school buddies.
We have barbecues in our backyards,
get drunk, go to the cottage,
get drunk, play golf, get drunk,
watch baseball on TV,
get drunk — none of us has any real plans.
We have our own indigenous way of life.
We are at home here.
Hey — we're white guys!
Nothin is a biggie...

As for the Africans — well, I don't know what happens to the
  Africans in summer.
You see, I don't want to know what happens to the Africans.
In principle, I am anti-apartheid, but in practice — well, it would
  be weird,
awkward, it's summer — the thing is, my high school pals, they
don't want to meet new people. They want things to be familiar.
Until
Late one night, around midnight, the phone rings,
— and it's Mabuti. Of all people.

Hey man, how are you? He asks.
Mabuti, how you doin'?
Thinking, why are you calling me in the summer?
I'm no good man.

Why not? What's wrong?
Thinking, please don't give me more information than I need?
I'm just not doing very good man, he says. I'm alone here.
You wanna go for a beer? He asks. You wanna do something?
Mabuti. I'm real tired.
One beer, man, he says. Come on.
I need company.
    [*Beat.*]
No, can't do it. I gotta get up early.
You take care, Mabuti. You'll be OK. 'Night!
I'm going to sleep now.
I can't go out drinking with everyone.
I gotta go to work in the morning.
I think these really normal thoughts everyone thinks all the time.
But I have another feeling, underneath those feelings.
Something like, that one was a test, a cosmic challenge.
And I failed.
In my own way, I said,
This is my house.
You can't come in.

BLACKOUT.

THE CHAIN LETTER

My new roommate is a guy who just got knifed in the heart.
He survived, but he's in critical condition.

Sal is six-two, a hundred and eighty pounds.
He's big — but he's Canadian.
He has posture like a question mark, like he didn't wanna be that tall,
and he's kinda mushy,
and he's got a bad roadie's ponytail,

and he's just thrilled
to live in the East Village
full of psychopaths & drug abusers
& unpublished poets.
No one is just who they are with Sal.
Everyone is this really big adjective.
Steve man, I met the most brilliant Jewish woman.
Richard is an astonishing poet, although he's really really depressed.
Molly is a fascinating crackhead. They're so complex.

His dad is a corporate lawyer and his mom works for the mayor
and they live in Vancouver on a house on a hill
and maybe that's why he loves living on Avenue B —

Every summer Sal leaves New York and goes back to Vancouver,
where he has a job,
licensing unlicensed pit bulls for the city.
At night he works as a bouncer in a nightclub.

Sal got knifed trying to help Donnie, the other bouncer.

ID please...[Beat.]
Sorry sailor, drinking age is twenty one in Vancouver.
Hey, you didn't know man.
Hey man. You can't come in.
Donnie — escort this guy down the ramp!

SHIT! Donnie! He's got a knife!
     [Beat.]
The guy starts cutting Donnie in the face.
Sal runs down the ramp
& gets the guy's arms pinned behind his back,
& for a moment, he seems to surrender.
Just long enough for Sal to relax his grip.
Then blade of that knife shines, and he sticks it into Sal.
Twice.
Then the guy runs.
Sal's t-shirt is covered with blood — which he thinks is Donnie's
blood.

Sal walks back up the ramp to get an ambulance for Donnie
when he notices
— the blood is his. Gushing out of him.

> SFX: *AMBULANCE SIRENS*
> SFX: *HEART MONITOR SOUNDS: 'BEEP'. 'BEEP'.*
> SFX: *WALKIE TALKIE DIALOGUE: "WE'RE LOSING*
> *HIM. WE'RE LOSING HIM ..."*
> SFX: *A LONGER, SLOWER 'BEEP' FROM THE*
> *HEART MONITOR.*
> SFX: *WALKIE TALKIE DIALOGUE; "WE LOST HIM".*

Lost him? Hey! Hello?
I'm not dead!
Hey!
Hey!
   [*Beat.*]
Heyyyy!!!!

In emergency, they cut open Sal's chest without anesthetic.
The doctor plunges a thumb into his heart, to shock it back to
    life.
It works.
Sal sits up on the table —

   [SAL *sits up.*]

I'm alive.

They perform emergency heart surgery on the spot.
They use fourteen pints of blood.
That's a lot of blood.
Think in terms of beer.

Sal makes it back to New York three weeks later, because he skips
out
on post-trauma therapy — and he doesn't wanna lose his sublet.
   [*Beat.*]

New York thing.
Sal doesn't doesn't wanna dwell on what happened to him.
He wants to move forward, get on with life, forget the past.
In Hanoi, the government prefers its citizens talk about the
    future,
not the past. The past is off limits, a forbidden zone.
Memories can be a dangerous thing.

Sal has plans.
He wants to write some really good short stories
and then get them published in a literary magazine
and then get a grant — Canadian thing —
and then get an agent
and then write a screenplay
and then make a lot of money —
Sal would be the darling of Hanoi.
But he's different now.
Around midnight, when he can't sleep,
he wakes me up.

Hey Steve, wanna grab a drink at the Mars Bar?
Are you tired? I'm not tired at all.
Ever since I got back, I can't sleep at all.
unless I get a couple drinks in me — are you sure you're tired?

He drinks Jack Daniels until three in the morning, so
that he can pass out until eight.
He tells me the things that happen to him.
Sal stalks people now.
He sees a guy getting in a fight with his girlfriend,
and he wants to kill the guy ...
He gets into huge arguments with complete strangers —
he doesn't care anymore about unpublished poets
or incomprehensible performance artists.
He's doing his own kind of social work now.

Hi Mom.
They caught him.
That's fantastic.

[*Beat.*]
What do you mean, aggravated assault?
The guy knifed me in the heart! Twice!
   [*Beat.*]
Well fuck the Navy and their white shoe attorney —
18 months!
You gotta be joking.
That's not a sentence — that's a fuckin' sabbatical.

So the guy gets out of jail, and Sal is still under his very own
   house arrest.

Sal looks at black people now and sees that guy with the knife.
Intellectually, he knows you can't blame a whole race
for something one guy did to you one night.
But now, I watch Sal, pacing our apartment at midnight,
wired and enraged,
and I realize something:
this is how hate grows.
It's like a chain letter of violence.
First you get it. Then you get it.
Then you give it to somebody else.
Until everybody's got their very own personal war wound.
And you know what that gets you, don't you?

It's midnight. There goes Sal.
Madder than hell. Out for a drink.
To see who he can run in to.

   BLACKOUT

CENTRAL PARK

The first time I meet Natalee, she's with her best friend Jennifer.
Jennifer is white, Nat is black.

"If Jennifer and me melted," she say, "We'd be Lisa Bonet!"
Nat went to Bennington College in Vermont,
loves Victorian architecture, and her favorite novel growing up
was *Anne of Green Gables*.
In high school, she dated Craig, who joined the Nation of Islam.

And then, a psychic told her she was destined to marry a writer.
The first time we went out, she said,
"Do you think you're destined to marry me?"
So I said, yes.
From the Nation of Islam — to me.

One day in August, we go for a picnic in Central Park.
We find a secluded spot in some trees, on the West Side,
around 82nd Street.
I open the wine. Natalee digs out the turkey sandwiches.
Classy turkey sandwiches: baguettes. Honey mustard.
Vine-ripened tomatoes with no street grit on them.
A real feast.
That's when a guy finds us and comes over — the way guys do in
    New York.
He looks OK. Not too dusty.

I haven't had anything to eat all day, he says, looking at me.
Could you give me something to eat please?

So I say, No.

Then he gives Nat a look.
Translated, it says something like, hey sister.
Seein' as you gave up on black men,
how's about a bite to eat for a struggling brother?

How about a pear? She asks, holding up a piece of fruit.
The guys takes the pear.

How about some real food, he says. How about a sandwich?

A pear is real, she says.

Besides, there's no extra sandwiches.
We're eating the only sandwiches we brought.
I worked all day, on my feet, from six-thirty in the morning
to six in the afternoon. I ate a bagel at seven-thirty, but that's it.
I'm not mad, but —
he ain't getting my sandwich.

How about a baguette, I ask. We have an extra.
You can have the whole thing.
How about a sandwich, he says again, like we never heard
the first time.
It's getting dark.
No one else is around.
We're in the middle of New York City and we're isolated —
and it's the urban nightmare: he won't take 'no' for an answer.

And that's when I give Nat a look.
Translated, it says,
He's your problem now, girlfriend!
And the weird, or sad, or inevitable thing
is that Nat looks at him like he is her problem.
She tears off half her sandwich, and holds it up to the guy —
And I'm thinking, maybe he won't take it,
Maybe he'll see
It's the only sandwich she brought —

But he takes it.
Says thank you.
Walks away.

After he's gone, we turn the whole episode into a kind of joke.
We are urban and detached about the whole deal.
How a pear wasn't real enough for him.
How he wouldn't take 'no' for an answer.
Nat says, "I felt like saying, 'Yo, brother, I spent my money on
    this.
I had to work for it. You don't look so bad. Somebody out there
would hire your sorry ass. Don't be badmouthing my food.'"

And I joke about these guys we run into all over Manhattan,
how every time they hear 'no' from me, they turn to Nat for
solidarity.
Thing is, they get it.

There are these episodes in the news.
Babies disappear and women go on the news and say, a black man
took my babies.
Happens down in South Carolina with Susan Smith, and up in
     Boston —
But it turns out, after investigating, that black men had nothing to
do with it.
These women were basically abducting themselves.
They just needed someone to blame.

One night, we're lying in bed, it's four AM, I have insomnia,
and Nat says,
I don't know if I should tell you this,
but Christina and me were talking about white people,
and Christina said,
"Ain't nothin' whiter than self-abduction."

I have to think about that one for a minute.

I mean, I think there are a few things whiter than self-abduction.
Like being on time.

I personally have never abducted myself.
But it was four AM logic, know what I'm sayin'?

And the radio is on, playing Grateful Dead music in honor of
Jerry Garcia, who just died young.

We sleep in this cubicle cut into the wall — it's very, very dark —
And I lie there, listening to the mandolin,
reflecting on a world where white people abduct themselves,
and blame black people,
and television networks get sold for $19 billion — the third place
network, yet! —

and when a guys yells at you on the street,
Hey baby, what's he got that I ain't got?
The answer, at the close of the twentieth century,
almost unbelievably, is:
a sandwich.

BLACKOUT

WHO'S MEDGAR EVARS?

The jury in the OJ Simpson trial has reached a verdict &
I'm sitting in the Dive Bar at 96th and Amsterdam Monday afternoon watching the Mariners — Angels playoff and all I'm thinking
is, thank god Randy Johnson isn't starting tomorrow against the
Yanks when they cut to an announcer who says the verdict will be
announced tomorrow, at one o'clock New York time.

Hang him, Marcia the bartender says.

The next day, it's one and I'm sitting in my chair listening to Mike
and the Mad Dog on WFAN when they cut live to Los Angeles for
the verdict.

I'm on the phone with Natalee.
Judge Ito comes on the radio.
I'm nervous.
I'm sure the verdict is gonna be guilty, and Nat is gonna be angry;
somehow, OJ Simpson cut off his wife's head and it's gonna end
up my fault.

Suprise.

When was the last time I was that suprised?
[Beat.]

Oh yeah.
I guess it was the last time a Los Angeles jury failed to convict.

Nat's on the other end of the line, cheering.
I knew it! I knew it would be not guilty! Justice is served! How many times has this scenario been played out the other way around? How many trials? This makes up for Medgar Evars! They caught his killers and you think they convicted them?

Who's Medgar Evars ? I ask.

There's silence on her end.
She says, *I'll forgive you for that because you're Canadian.*

I'm stunned. I'm not breathing properly. It's Tuesday afternoon, and it's like there's been a total eclipse of the sun:
Everything just stops.

But I'm not mad. Well, maybe a little mad. OK. I'm mad. But I don't wanna be — because I don't want the issue of OJ's innocence or guilt to become the defining moment of our relationship — because I like our relationship. We basically have a great relationship. We have a lot of laughs, and there's drama everyday, and we still manage to find the romance in life. We both like mornings, and going for walks and she makes me forget I'm poor and if I wake up before she does in the morning, sometimes I just lie there, and watch her sleep, and that makes me feel lucky.
If we broke up because of some fight over that dopey OJ, I would feel so stupid, I think I would cut my own head off.

I have perspective on this, because it almost happened.
The week before the verdict, Nat meets my sister for the first time at a Japanese restaurant in the East Village. My sister is a lawyer, as is her best friend Lori, who joins us for dinner. They both talk about OJ because it's all about lawyers. Nat talks about it, because it matters to her to get along with my family. I don't talk about, because I don't want anyone to start fighting — so I just sit there and

scarf down sushi and beer and pray no one gets mad — and no one does, basically because Nat doesn't quite address the two solitudes that represent black and white perspectives on this trial.

Nat is caught, in her own eyes, between being a good girlfriend and a good black person — someone who doesn't just fit in and get along so that everybody at the table can almost forget she's black.
I know this, because she tells me, the next day in one of her famous phone monologues.
She has been sitting home all day feeling as if she betrayed her race again, because she didn't speak up the night before. She doesn't like black people who act like they're not black. She feels guilty about being so non-threatening to white people.
She's determined to be more assertive about her African-American identity.
She's so determined, on the last night my sister's in town, she won't go out for dinner with us.

Now I'm mad.

We go out and have a perfectly great time, and she's not there.
For no reason at all.
She's home, being a good black person.
Not assimilating.
Or whatever.
But I don't care.
Because it isn't just any old white people she's not assimilating with.
It's me.
I ride the subway back uptown thinkin', if going out for dinner with my family
makes you a bad black person,
maybe you just better find yourself some brother you can hang out with their
family any time you like.
But! I'm also an emotional coward.
So the next day, I tell her I was mad, but now I'm kind of detached from my anger — as if it was random anger I found somewhere.
Nothing personal.

And she's the same way.
When I confront her on it, it starts to sound more like a money issue —
she's broke, and I bought sushi the night before, and she felt guilty or uncertain,
or wasn't quite clear whether I wanted her to be there or not, and
of course, I wasn't clear, because I'm never clear — not even to
       myself —
Until, I feel so relieved!
She's just like all my ex-girlfriends!
We just don't communicate!

The night of the verdict, she goes to Naked Angels , which she does every Tuesday, and participates in a reading.
I can't go — Yankees game.
I've never been so relieved to go to a Yankees game.
Everyone's gonna be talking about the verdict — and I don't wanna go there.
Because I'm having this feeling: no matter what I have to say about OJ, I can't win.

After Naked Angels, everyone goes to Nadine's for drinks, and Nat gets into a huge argument with five white guys about the verdict. Who say what I haven't had the nerve to say.

At 2:30 in the morning, here she comes, up the steps into the apartment.
I have Delayed Reaction Syndrome, she says.
So it took until now to get mad about something Alan said.
Alan said, you go out with a white guy because of your self-loathing as a black person.

Lately, I feel like a fireman.
Like my purpose on this earth is to douse out the flames
that keep breaking out between people.

The other day, I was reading the paper about Bosnia and it was about how there were now Serbian refugees and I got this weird feeling in my gut — because there was no longer a clear-cut bad guy. It was the Serbs — but now they were refugees.

And the thing about people is often, there is no clear-cut villain. Because we're all equally capable of evil. It's like Janis Joplin once tried to describe time by saying, *It's all the same fuckin' day anyway*.

Sometimes, you know what I think?

I think, *We're all the same fuckin' person!*

I'm thinking, thinking, thinking: how are we gonna make it through this?

'Know what you tell Alan?' I ask.

'What?

"Tell him you go out with me because of your self-loathing — as an *American*."

BLACKOUT

ETHNIC PRODUCTS

IT'S A RAINY SUNDAY NIGHT IN NOVEMBER, Nat needs to wash her hair and she's out of shampoo. She has a job tomorrow, working in Century City for the people who produced 'Caspar the Friendly Ghost.' She has no driver's license yet, so I volunteer to drive to the Rite Aid drugs at Wilshire & 14th to get some more.

Two weeks earlier, on a Tuesday afternoon in November, in Norwalk, a nowhere strip mall town off the I-5, we stand before a Justice of the Peace, in a meeting room-turned Chapel, under a makeshift wreath, and promise to love, honor, respect — and we finally do it.

We get married.

Nat looks beautiful, in a white, silk slip dress, our friend- and witness – Monica takes pictures with a disposable fifteen buck cardboard camera, and after years of swearing I'd never marry anyone I'm shocked to report —

I feel happy.

They're making drugstores bigger these days.
They sell a lot of things drugstores never used to sell — like food.
It would be better for everyone if I just asked for help, but for some unknown, deeply genetic reason I won't.

I'm a husband now.

Instead, I drift haphazardly towards Hair Care.
Thinking, this is one of those situations where if you're not careful, you end up with screams and tears and doors slamming —
Because not only am I buying women's hair care, I'm buying black women's hair care products —
And black women have all these hair issues.
For so long, black women have experienced, in American culture, a kind of ongoing hair attack. You know, every commercial on television is like, Silky&Smooth, Breezy&Bouncy, Long&Straight, Pert, Perky and you can pretty much bet the house on blonde.
Not too many commercials about black, curly, wiry & wild.

Nat has this gigantic afro. It's very Seventies. When she wakes up in the morning, sometimes, it's all bent —
I love her afro. To me, her afro is just like she is — spontaneous, unpredictable, a journey from which you return a changed man.

As far as Nat is concerned, it would be ideal if I just never found out about her hair products — she would prefer they stay all mysterious and secretive,
like Stonehenge.

I locate Hair Care, and carefully eyeball each shelf, determined to choose correctly. Nat wrote a whole list of acceptable products — a list I seem to have misplaced.
Although I sort of remember them.
Texturizer. Structuralizer. Relaxer.
Only ...

None of those products I need are located in the shampoo section, as far as I can tell. To tell you the truth, I don't even know if they are shampoo, or what they are ... these mysterious black people's hair care products.

Until I turn a corner and look up.

And hanging from the ceiling of the store is a sign describing what they they have for sale on this aisle.

They've managed to narrow this aisle I'm standing in down to a single, two word description.

Ethnic Products.

I think I'm getting warm!

Ethnic Products look collectively like a lot of things invented in the '50's that you might hear advertised on a Brooklyn Dodgers radio broadcast, products like Burma After Shave — not something for sale in a Rite Aid in 1998.

There's Pomade gel. De-Curling spray. Skin lightner.

Finally, paydirt. A box of texturizer. That's the stuff.

I go to the cashier, and put the texturizer on the counter, really quick and low key, hoping the cashier doesn't think I'm some sort of fetishist, a white guy buying ethnic products to rub all over his body on a rainy Sunday night in West L. A.

When I realize something.

I have this epiphany of sorts.

They're all ethnic products, aren't they?

Every last single damn aisle.

Bass Ale.

Sushi.

Khaki shorts.

An hour later, Nat steps out of the shower all clean and fresh and sits down next to me. I'm eating takeout oysters and watching TV. Tonight, on the "Wonderful World of Disney," it's 'Cinderella' — starring Brandy, a nappy-haired black girl playing Cinderella. Whoopi Goldberg plays Cinderella's step-mom and a vaguely Asian-looking guy of some indeterminate ethnicity plays Prince Charming.

Nat and me sit and watch the fairy tale unfold, until I blurt out that I think Brandy is funny-looking.

Nat says, "I don't. I think it's great that somewhere in America tonight, some nappy-headed black girl gets to turn on TV and see someone who looks just like her playing the most beautiful girl at the ball, because that's sure not the same TV I grew up watching."

And then I realize something: that nappy-headed black girl she's talking about
might be my *daughter.*

Sitting there in a white terrycloth robe, my very own Cinderella says,
"Make yourself useful. Pass me the damn oysters."

BLACKOUT

THE END

David Ives

TIME FLIES

David Ives

David Ives was born in Chicago and educated at Northwestern University and Yale School of Drama. A 1995 Guggenheim Fellow in playwriting, he is probably best known for *All In The Timing*, an evening of one-act comedies first produced by Primary Stages in New York and, subsequently, in Chicago, San Francisco, Seattle, Dallas, Philadelphia, Washington, St. Louis, Berlin, Vienna, and Sydney, among many other places here and abroad. *All In The Timing* was awarded an Outer Circle Award for playwriting, was nominated for a Drama Desk Award for best play, was included in *The Best American Short Plays of 1993-94*, and was the most-performed play nationally (except for Shakespeare productions) in the 1995-96 season. Other plays by David Ives include: *Don Juan In Chicago*; *Ancient History*; *The Land of Cocaigne*; the short plays *English Made Simple*; *Seven Menus*; *Foreplay or the Art of the Fugue*; *Mere Mortals*; *Long Ago and Far Away*; and an opera, *The Secret Garden*, which premiered at the Pennsylvania Opera Theatre. Two other of his short plays have also appeared in the *Best American Short Plays* series; *Degas, C'est Moi* in the *1995-96* edition, and *Sure Thing*, included in the *Best American Short Plays of 1990*.

This play Is for John Rando, Anne O'Sullivan, Arnie Burton, and Willis Sparks who made it fly

CHARACTERS:

HORACE

MAY

DAVID ATTENBOROUGH

A FROG

[*Evening. A pond. The* CHIRR *of treetoads, and the* BUZZ *of a huge swarm of* INSECTS. *Upstage, a thicket of tall* CATTAILS. *Downstage, a* DEEP GREEN LOVESEAT. *Overhead, an* ENORMOUS FULL MOON.*].

[*A* LOUD CUCKOO SOUNDS, *like the mechanical "cuckoo" of a clock.*]

Lights come up on two MAYFLIES: HORACE *and* MAY, *buzzing as they "fly" in. They are dressed like singles on an evening out, he in a jacket and tie, she in a party dress — but they have insect-like antennae; long tube-like tails; and on their backs, translucent wings. Outsized hornrim glasses give the impression of very large eyes.* MAY *has distinctly hairy legs.*

HORACE & MAY: Bzzzzzzzzzzzzzzzzzz ...

[*Their wings stop fluttering, as they "settle."*]

MAY: Well here we are. This is my place.

HORACE: Already? That was fast.

MAY: Swell party, huh.

HORACE: Yeah. Quite a swarm.

MAY: Thank you for flying me home.

HORACE: No. Sure. I'm happy to. Absolutely. My pleasure. I mean — you're very, very, very welcome.

[*Their eyes lock and they near each other as if for a kiss, their wings fluttering a little.*]

HORACE: [*Cont'd.*] Bzzzzzzzz ...

MAY: Bzzzzzzzz ...

[*Before their jaws can meet: "CUCKOO!" — and* HORACE *breaks away.*]

HORACE: It's that late, is it. Anyway, it was very nice meeting you — I'm sorry, is it April?

MAY: May.

HORACE: May. Yes. Later than I thought, huh.

[*They laugh politely.*]

MAY: That's very funny, Vergil.

HORACE: It's Horace, actually.

MAY: I'm sorry. The buzz at that party was so loud.

HORACE: So you're "May the mayfly."

MAY: Yeah. Guess my parents didn't have much imagination. May, mayfly.

HORACE: You don't, ah, live with your parents, do you, May?

MAY: No, my parents died around dawn this morning.

HORACE: Isn't that funny. Mine died around dawn too.

MAY: Maybe it's fate.

HORACE: Is that what it izzzzzzzz…?

MAY: Bzzzzzzzz…

HORACE: Bzzzzzzzzzzzzz…[*They near for a kiss, but* HORACE *breaks away*.] Well I'd better be going now. Good night.

MAY: Do you want a drink?

HORACE: I'd love a drink, actually …

MAY: Let me just turn on a couple of fireflies.

> [MAY *tickles the underside of a couple of* TWO FOOT-LONG FIREFLIES *hanging like a chandelier, and the* FIREFLIES LIGHT UP.]

HORACE: Wow. Great pond! [*Indicating the* LOVESEAT:] I love the lilypad.

MAY: That was here. It kinda grew on me. [*Polite laugh*.] Care to take the load off your wings?

HORACE: That's all right. I'll just — you know — hover. But will you look at that…!

> [*Turning,* HORACE *bats* MAY *with his wings.*]

MAY: Oof!

HORACE: I'm sorry. Did we collide?

MAY: No. No. It's fine.

HORACE: I've only had my wings about six hours.

MAY: Really! So have I...! Wasn't molting disgusting?

HORACE: Eugh. I'm glad that's over.

MAY: Care for some music? I've got The Beatles, The Byrds, The Crickets...

HORACE: I love the Crickets.

MAY: Well so do I...

[*She* KICKS *a* LARGE, INSECT-SHAPED COFFEE TABLE, *and we hear the* BUZZ *of* CRICKETS.]

HORACE: [*As they boogie to that.*] So are you going out with any — I mean, are there any other mayflies in the neighborhood?

MAY: No, it's mostly wasps.

HORACE: So, you live here by your, um, all by yourself? Alone?

MAY: All by my lonesome.

HORACE: And will you look at that moon.

MAY: You know that's the first moon I've ever seen?

HORACE: That's the first moon I've ever seen...!

MAY: Isn't that funny.

HORACE: When were you born?

MAY: About 7:30 this morning.

HORACE: So was I! Seven thirty-three!

MAY: Isn't that funny.

HORACE: Or maybe it's fate. [*They near each other again, as if for a kiss:*] Bzzzzzzz ...

MAY: Bzzzzzzzzz...I think that moon is having a very emotional effect on me.

HORACE: Me too.

MAY: It must be nature.

HORACE: Me too.

MAY: Or maybe it's fate.

HORACE: Me too...

MAY: Bzzzzzzzzzz...

HORACE: Bzzzzzzzzzzzzzz...

[*They draw their tails very close. Suddenly:*]

A FROG: [*Amplified, over loudspeaker.*] Ribbit, ribbit!

HORACE: A frog!

MAY: A frog!

HORACE & MAY: The frogs are coming, the frogs are coming! [*They "fly" around the stage in a panic. Ad lib:*] A frog, a frog! The frogs are coming, the frogs are coming!

[*They finally stop, breathless.*]

MAY: It's okay. It's okay.

HORACE: Oh my goodness.

MAY: I think he's gone now.

HORACE: Oh my goodness, that scared me.

MAY: That is the only drawback to living here. The frogs.

HORACE: You know I like frog films and frog literature. I just don't like frogs.

MAY: And they're so rude if you're not a frog yourself.

HORACE: Look at me. I'm shaking.

MAY: Why don't I fix you something. Would you like a grasshopper? Or a stinger?

HORACE: Just some stagnant water would be fine.

MAY: A little duckweed in that? Some algae?

HORACE: Straight up is fine.

MAY: [*As she pours his drink.*] Sure I couldn't tempt you to try the lily pad?

HORACE: Well, maybe for just a second.

[HORACE *flutters down onto the love seat:*]

Zzzzzzz...

MAY: [*Handing him a glass.*] Here you go. Cheers, Horace.

HORACE: Long life, May.

[*They clink glasses.*]

MAY: Do you want to watch some tube?

HORACE: Sure. What's on?

MAY: Let's see. [*She checks a GREEN TV GUIDE.*] There is… "*The Love Bug,*" "*M. Butterfly,*" "*The Spider's Stratagem,*" "*Travels With My Ant,*" "*Angels and Insects,*" "*The Fly*"…

HORACE: The original, or Jeff Goldblum?

MAY: Jeff Goldblum.

HORACE: Euch. Too gruesome.

MAY: "Born Yesterday" And "Life On Earth."

HORACE: What's on that?

MAY: "Swamp Life," with Sir David Attenborough.

HORACE: That sounds good.

MAY: Shall we try it?

HORACE: Carpe diem.

MAY: Carpe diem? What's that?

HORACE: I don't know. It's Latin.

MAY: What's Latin?

HORACE: I don't know. I'm just a mayfly.

[*"Cuckoo!"*]

And we're right on time for it.

[MAY *presses a* REMOTE CONTROL *and* DAVID ATTENBOROUGH *appears, wearing a safari jacket.*]

DAVID ATTENBOROUGH: Hello, I'm David Attenborough. Welcome to "Swamp Life."

MAY: Isn't this comfy.

HORACE: Is my wing in your way?

MAY: No. It's fine.

DAVID ATTENBOROUGH: You may not believe it, but within this seemingly lifeless puddle, there thrives a teeming world of vibrant life.

HORACE: May, look — isn't that your pond?

MAY: I think that is my pond!

HORACE: He said "puddle."

DAVID ATTENBOROUGH: This puddle is only several inches across, but its stagnant water plays host to over 14 gazillion different species.

MAY: It is my pond!

DAVID ATTENBOROUGH: Every species here is engaged in a constant, desperate battle for survival. Feeding — meeting — mating — breeding — dying. And mating. And meeting. And mating. And feeding. And dying. Mating. Mating. Meeting.

Breeding. Brooding. Braiding — those that can braid. Feeding. Mating.

MAY: All right, Sir Dave!

DAVID ATTENBOROUGH: Mating, mating, mating, and mating.

HORACE: Only one thing on his mind.

MAY: The filth on television these days.

DAVID ATTENBOROUGH: Tonight we start off with one of the saddest creatures of this environment.

HORACE: The dung beetle.

MAY: The toad.

DAVID ATTENBOROUGH: The lowly mayfly.

HORACE: Did he say "the mayfly?"

MAY: I think he said the lowly mayfly.

DAVID ATTENBOROUGH: Yes. The lowly mayfly. Like these two mayflies, for instance.

HORACE: May — I think that's us!

MAY: Oh my God ...

HORACE & MAY: [*Together.*] We're on television!

HORACE: I don't believe it!

MAY: I wish my mother was here to see this!

HORACE: This is amazing!

MAY: Oh God, I look terrible!

HORACE: You look very good.

MAY: I can't look at this.

DAVID ATTENBOROUGH: As you can see, the lowly mayfly is not one of nature's most attractive creatures.

MAY: At least we don't wear safari jackets.

HORACE: I wish he'd stop saying "lowly mayfly."

DAVID ATTENBOROUGH: The lowly mayfly has a very distinctive khkhkhkhkhkhkhkhkhkkh…[— *the sound of TV "static.*]

MAY: I think there's something wrong with my antenna…[*She adjusts the antenna on her head.*]

HORACE: You don't have cable?

MAY: Not on this pond.

DAVID ATTENBOROUGH: [*Stops the static sound.*]…and sixty tons of droppings.

HORACE: That fixed it.

MAY: Can I offer you some food? I've got some plankton in the pond. And some very nice gnat.

HORACE: I do love good gnat.

MAY: I'll set it out, you can pick.

[*She rises and gets some food, as:*]

DAVID ATTENBOROUGH: The lowly mayfly first appeared some 350 million years ago...

MAY: That's impressive.

DAVID ATTENBOROUGH: ...and is of the order Ephemeroptera, meaning, "living for a single day."

MAY: I did not know that!

HORACE: "Living for a single day." Huh...

MAY: [*Setting out a tray on the coffee table.*] There you go.

HORACE: Gosh, May. That's beautiful.

MAY: There's curried gnat, salted gnat, Scottish smoked gnat...

HORACE: I love that.

MAY: ...gnat with pesto, gnat au naturelle, and Gnat King Cole.

HORACE: I don't think I could finish a whole one.

MAY: "Gnat" to worry. [*They laugh politely.*] That's larva dip there in the center. Just dig in.

DAVID ATTENBOROUGH: As for the life of the common mayfly ...

HORACE: Oh. We're "common" now.

DAVID ATTENBOROUGH: ...it is a simple round of meeting, mating, meeting, mating —

MAY: Here we go again.

DAVID ATTENBOROUGH: — breeding, feeding, feeding ...

HORACE: This dip is fabulous.

DAVID ATTENBOROUGH: ...and dying.

MAY: Leaf?

HORACE: Thank you.

[MAY *breaks a* LEAF *off a* PLANT *and hands it to* HORACE.]

DAVID ATTENBOROUGH: Mayflies are a major food source for trout and salmon.

MAY: Will you look at that savagery?

HORACE: That poor, poor mayfly.

DAVID ATTENBOROUGH: Fishermen like to bait hooks with mayfly lookalikes.

MAY: Bastards! — Excuse me.

DAVID ATTENBOROUGH: And then there is the giant bullfrog.

FROG: [*Amplified, over* LOUDSPEAKER] Ribbit, ribbit!

HORACE & MAY: The frogs are coming, the frogs are coming!

[*They "fly" around the stage in a panic — and end up "flying" right into each other's arms.*]

HORACE: Well there.

MAY: Hello.

DAVID ATTENBOROUGH: Welcome to "Swamp Life."

[DAVID ATTENBOROUGH *exits*.]

MAY: [*Hypnotized by* HORACE.] Funny how we flew right into each other's wings.

HORACE: It is funny.

MAY: Or fate.

HORACE: Do you think he's gone?

MAY: David Attenborough?

HORACE: The frog.

MAY: What frog? Bzzzz...

HORACE: Bzzzzz...

DAVID ATTENBOROUGH'S VOICE: As you see, mayflies can be quite affectionate...

HORACE & MAY: Bzzzzzzzzzzz...

DAVID ATTENBOROUGH'S VOICE: ...mutually palpating their proboscises.

HORACE: You know I've been wanting to palpate your proboscis all evening?

MAY: I think it was larva at first sight.

HORACE & MAY: [*Rubbing proboscises together.*]

Zzzzzzzzzzzzzzzzzzzzzzzzzzzz...

MAY: [*very British, "Brief Encounter."*] Oh darling, darling.

HORACE: Oh do darling do let's always be good to each other, shall we?

MAY: Let's do do that, darling, always, always.

HORACE: Always?

MAY: Always.

HORACE & MAY: Zzzzzzzzzzzzzzzzzzzzzzzzzzzzzzzzz!

MAY: Rub my antennae. Rub my antennae.

[HORACE *rubs* MAY'S *antennae with his hands.*]

DAVID ATTENBOROUGH'S VOICE: Sometimes mayflies rub antennae together.

MAY: Oh yes. Yes. Just like that. Yes. Keep going. Harder. Rub harder.

HORACE: Rub mine now. Rub my antennae. Oh yes. Yes. Yes. Yes. There's the rub. There's the rub. Go. Go. Go!

DAVID ATTENBOROUGH'S VOICE: Isn't that a picture. Now get a load of mating.

[HORACE *gets into mounting position, behind* MAY. *He rubs her antennae while she wolfs down the gnat-food in front of her.*]

HORACE & MAY: Bzzzzzzzzzzzzzzzzzzzzzzzzzzzzzzzzzzzzzz!

DAVID ATTENBOROUGH'S VOICE: Unfortunately for this insect, the mayfly has a lifespan of only one day.

[HORACE *and* MAY *stop buzzing, abruptly.*]

HORACE: What was that...?

DAVID ATTENBOROUGH'S VOICE: The mayfly has a lifespan of only one day — living just long enough to meet, mate, have off-spring, and die.

MAY: Did he say "meet, mate, have offspring, and DIE" — ?

DAVID ATTENBOROUGH'S VOICE: I did. In fact, mayflies born at 7:30 in the morning will die by the next dawn.

HORACE: [*Whimpers softly at the thought.*]

DAVID ATTENBOROUGH'S VOICE: But so much for the lowly mayfly. Let's move on to the newt.

[*"Cuckoo!"*]

HORACE & MAY: We're going to die...We're going to die! Mayday, mayday! We're going to die, we're going to die! [*Weeping and wailing, they kneel, beat their breasts, cross themselves, daven, and tear their hair.*]

[*"Cuckoo!"*]

HORACE: What time is it? What time is it?

MAY: I don't wear a watch. I'm a lowly mayfly!

HORACE: [*Weeping.*] Wah-ha-ha-ha!

MAY: [*Suddenly sober.*] Well isn't this beautiful.

HORACE: [*Gasping for breath.*] Oh my goodness. I think I'm having an asthma attack. Can mayflies have asthma?

MAY: I don't know. Ask Mr. Safari Jacket.

HORACE: Maybe if I put a paper bag over my head…

MAY: So this is my sex life?

HORACE: Do you have a paper bag?

MAY: One bang, a bambino, and boom — that's it?

HORACE: Do you have a paper bag?

MAY: For the common mayfly, foreplay segues right into funeral.

HORACE: Do you have a paper bag?

MAY: I don't have time to look for a paper bag, I'm going to be dead very shortly, all right?

[*"Cuckoo!"*]

HORACE: Oh come on! That wasn't a whole hour!

[*"Cuckoo!"*]

Time is moving so fast now.

[*"Cuckoo!"*]

HORACE & MAY: Shut up!

[*"Cuckoo!"*]

HORACE: [*Suddenly sober.*] This explains everything. We were born this morning, we hit puberty in mid-afternoon, our biological clocks went BONG, and here we are. Hot to copulate.

MAY: For the one brief miserable time we get to do it.

HORACE: Yeah.

MAY: Talk about a quickie.

HORACE: Wait a minute, wait a minute.

MAY: Talk fast.

HORACE: What makes you think it would be so brief?

MAY: Oh, I'm sorry. Did I insult your vast sexual experience?

HORACE: Are you more experienced than I am, Dr. Ruth? Luring me here to your pad?

MAY: I see. I see. Blame me!

HORACE: Can I remind you we only get one shot at this?

MAY: So I can rule out multiple orgasms, is that it?

HORACE: I'm just saying there's not a lot of time to hone one's erotic technique, okay?

MAY: Hmp!

HORACE: And I'm trying to sort out some very big entomontological questions here rather quickly, do you mind?

MAY: And I'm just the babe here, is that it? I'm just a piece of tail.

HORACE: I'm not the one who suggested TV.

MAY: I'm not the one who wanted to watch "Life On Earth." "Oh — Swamp Life. That sounds interesting."

FROG: Ribbit, ribbit.

HORACE: [*Calmly.*] There's a frog up there.

MAY: Oh, I'm really scared. I'm terrified.

FROG: Ribbit, ribbit!

HORACE: [*Calling to the frog.*] We're right down here! Come and get us!

MAY: Breeding. Dying. Breeding. Dying. So this is the whole purpose of mayflies? To make more mayflies?

HORACE: Does the world need more mayflies?

MAY: We're a major food source for trout and salmon.

HORACE: How nice for the salmon.

MAY: Do you want more food?

HORACE: I've lost a bit of my appetite, all right?

MAY: Oh. Excuse me.

HORACE: I'm sorry. Really, May.

MAY: [*Starts to cry.*] Males!

HORACE: Leaf? [*He plucks another LEAF and hands it to her.*]

MAY: Thank you.

HORACE: Really. I didn't mean to snap at you.

MAY: Oh, you've been very nice.

[*"CUCKOO!" They jump.*]

Under the circumstances.

HORACE: I'm sorry.

MAY: No, I'm sorry.

HORACE: No, I'm sorry.

MAY: No, I'm sorry.

HORACE: No, I'm sorry.

MAY: We'd better stop apologizing, we're going to be dead soon.

HORACE: I'm sorry.

MAY: Oh Horace, I had such plans. I had such wonderful plans. I wanted to see Paris.

HORACE: What's Paris?

MAY: I have no fucking idea.

HORACE: Maybe we'll come back as caviar and find out. [*They laugh a little at that.*] I was just hoping to live till Tuesday.

MAY: [*Making a small joke*] What's a Tuesday? [*They laugh a little more at that.*] The sun's going to be up soon. I'm scared, Horace. I'm so scared.

HORACE: You know, May, we don't have much time, and really, we hardly know each other — but I'm going to say it. I think you're swell. I think you're divine. From your buggy eyes to the thick raspy hair on your legs to the intoxicating scent of your secretions.

MAY: Eeeuw.

HORACE: Eeeuw? No. I say woof. And I say who cares if life is a swamp and we're just a couple of small bugs in a very small pond. I say live, May! I say...darn it...live!

MAY: But how?

HORACE: Well I don't honestly know that...

[ATTENBOROUGH *appears*.]

DAVID ATTENBOROUGH: You could fly to Paris.

MAY: We could fly to Paris!

HORACE: Do we have time to fly to Paris?

MAY: Carpe diem!

HORACE: What is carpe diem?

DAVID ATTENBOROUGH: It means "bon voyage."

HORACE & MAY: And we're outta here!

[*They fly off to Paris as...*]

[*Blackout.*]

THE END

Lavonne Mueller

THE CONFESSION OF MANY STRANGERS

(BASED ON THE LIFE OF THE PILOT OF THE ENOLA GAY)

*The poems I read tonight, written forty or
twenty-five years ago, did I really write them?
Am I the same? This book has been written by
a succession of poets: all have vanished and all that
remains of them are their words. My poetic
biography is made of the confession of many strangers.*

Octavio Paz

Lavonne Mueller

Lavonne Mueller's play, *Lettters To A Daughter From Prison*, about Nehru and his daughter, Indira, was produced at the First International Festival of the Arts in New York City and went on to tour in India. Her play, *Violent Peace*, was produced in London in 1992 and was the "Critics Choice" in *Time Out* Magazine. Her play, *Little Victories*, was produced by the Women's Project in New York City and was later produced in Tokyo by Theatre Classic Productions and directed by Riho Mitachi. Her play, *The Only Woman General* was produced by the Women's Project and starred Colleen Dewhurst and later went on to the Edinburgh Festival where it was "Pick of the Fringe." She was awarded the Roger Stevens Playwriting Award at the Kennedy Center in 1992. She is a Woodrow Wilson Scholar, a Lila Wallace Reader's Digest Writing Fellow, and has received a Guggenheim Grant, a Rockefeller Grant, three National Endowment for the Arts Grants, a Fulbright to Argentina, an Asian Culture Council Grant to Calcutta, and a U.S. Friendship Commission Grant to Japan. Her plays have been published by Dramatist Play Service, Samuel French, Applause Books, Theatre Communication Group, Heinemann Books and Baker's Plays. Her textbook, *Creative Writing*, published by Doubleday and The National Textbook Company is used by students around the world. She taught at Columbia University for five years. As a Woodrow Wilson Visiting Scholar, she helped colleges around the United States set up writing programs. She has been an Arts America speaker for the United States Information Service in India, Finland, Romania, Japan, the former Yugoslavia, and Norway. She was a Fulbright Fellow to Jordan and also received a National Endowment for the Humanities Grant to do research in Paris during the summer of 1995. She has been a writing fellow at the Edward Albee Foundation, the Djerassi Foundation, Hawthorden Castle and Funduncio Valperasio in Spain. Her play, *American Dreamers*, was selected for *Best American Short Plays, 1995-96*. This play, *The Confession of Many Strangers*, was produced at Lucille Lortel's The White Barn Theatre starring Tony LoBianco.

PLACE: *The Smithsonian Air and Space Museum, Washington, D.C., August 1995.*

[*Light up on a chair over on its side. After a beat, we see the* PILOT *strut proudly onto the stage. He is wearing full military dress with medals including the distinguished service cross.*]

PILOT: [*He looks all around him and then sees his airplane.*]
     My...*Enola Gay*

[*Turns to see spectators in the museum looking at the Enola Gay.*]

Glad to see some patriotic folks here. That's right. I'm the pilot. The one who flew her over Hiroshima. The uniform's the same, a little tight under the arms, but that's about all. Come on, stand a little closer. It's all right to gawk at the *Enola*. She's named after my mother. Yah, my mother. [*A beat.*] Quite a smooth nose on her. And slim. Gently curved tail section. Two wings like bosoms.

[*A beat.*]

It never bothers me that people know mom's name and not mine. She did all the work. Raised me. Gave me faith to fly.

[*To* MUSEUM SPECTATOR:]

I know it will surprise you, but that historic mission was so ordinary it was almost boring. Except...except...*after* the bomb dropped. Then things changed. The *Enola* took shock waves slamming us from nine miles away. I thought we were hit. It was like a huge giant had slapped us with a two by four. All we could do was hold on. I didn't know if the windows of our pressurized cabin would blow. On top of that, we got an "echo wave" coming off the first blast. We were rocking like there was artillery coming at us from everywhere. For one split second, I thought the atmosphere had exploded. Remember, we didn't exactly know what to expect. We'd never dropped an A-Bomb from a plane — the test bomb at Trinity was dropped from a tower. We were all working in the dark.

[*A beat.*]

I'll tell you straight out, when just a few people knew what

I did that day, right after I got back, I felt in control. Because I could go and have a beer and talk to each one of those people and tell them how I saved a lot of lives. Now...what I did is everybody's story. People just think and say whatever they want about me. I'm here to give you the truth.

[*He turns the chair over and sits on it. He takes a blank sheet of paper out of his pocket and makes an airplane.*]

[*He sails the paper plane out into the audience.*]

I was supposed to be a doctor. But being up next to somebody...getting so close you could see their cells...that felt kinda disrespectful. I like distance. There's dignity in seeing the long view. You don't get the warts. What I do I wanna do at least 10,000 feet up. [*A beat.*] I read somewhere that I supposedly learned to fly when I was five. On the knee of an old farmer who took me up in his home-made crate. Hell, how stupid can you get? Five! I didn't fly till I was ten.

[*To the audience:*]

You see, I had just met Earl Ebberly over in Paw Paw, Illinois. Earl had himself an old biplane called *Wilma* with wooden propellers and an open cockpit. The lift-strut on *The Wilma* was a head-board from his mother's bed. [*A beat.*] Earl let me do little jobs for him like picking up oil rags. One day he let me sit in the open cockpit just so I could get the feel of things. Earl saw me smiling and posing like somebody out of Battle Aces, and that's when he said he had this contract with the Army to test tropical chocolate bars by dropping them over state fairs and racetracks to see how they'd hold up. And he needed somebody to do the dropping while he did the flying. Was I interested? [*A beat.*] Was I interested!!

[*To the audience:*]

Instead of going to school where we were studying "percents," I left a note for the teacher. "Dear Miss Tidewalker, have gone flying." [*A beat.*] Flying was pretty primitive in those days. Earl made a flight line on the ground with the twig from a Spruce tree. He lined up some flour sacks on two sides for the runway. And then he just picked up that plane by the tail and pulled it along behind him and came right up to where I was standing. And I thought then and there...nothing...nothing in this whole world could be more grand than...[*He drags the chair by the back across the stage.*]...walking across a dirt patch in the middle of Illinois pulling your own airplane behind you.

[*A beat.*]

That first day Earl and me went up, we took off into low, broken cloud layers with a clear blue sky. I could smell gasoline. Oil was lashing back all over us. The air pounded my face, but I just put out my arms [*He does this.*] and let the wind blow them back like I was part of that plane.

[*To the audience:*]

Each candy bar was attached to a little parachute. I'd lean over real careful and take two handfuls of them candy bars and make a precision aim...and I swear they all floated down smooth and straight right on target.

[To EARL]

Earl, what if you get sick or pass out or something up here. What will I do?

[*Speaking as* EARL:]

Kid, lean on the stick and pump hard on the rudder pedals. If you don't have any hands left to drop the candy, do a slow roll all the way over and let them just fall out.

[*To* EARL:]

Sure, Earl, guess I can do that. [*To the audience:*] We flew over fairs, rodeos, firemen, picnics, and baseball games. Even over a pig-calling contest in Sabbona, Illinois.

[*In the airplane dropping candy bars:*]

Look at everybody run to get our chocolate bars, Earl. They're laughing. Pushing and shoving. Screaming. Ok...ok...more coming. These...are going...right over the Tilt-A-Whirl. [*He drops more candy bars.*]

[*To the audience:*]

Earl taught me to fly.

Course I learned to fly officially when I enlisted and became a second Looie in the Army Air Corps.

[*A beat.*]

I guess everybody remembers where they were when they heard about Pearl Harbor. I was at a party at the Officers Club. A good buddy and his wife invited a single woman friend of theirs to make a foursome. I had dated off and on over the years, but one look at Jenny, and I knew it was serious. [*A beat.*] I was pretty cocky then. We were out on the dance floor. Sammy Kaye was playing something smooth but with a swing. "*Why Don't We Do This More Often.*"

[*To* JENNY:]

[*He does the two-step and sings. Then:*] Courting a girl is like being on a runway —ready for flight. [*He does a little motion with his right hands to twirl her around as he sings. Then:*]

First, your clear for take-off with a flower.

[*He gives* JENNY *a flower.*]

[*To* JENNY:]

Next…dinner and dancing, honey. That will taxi us out.

One kiss. Gets us up 5,000 feet.

A little lover's quarrel. That brings on a stall.

Hug and make up, baby.

Engagement ring. Landed. [*He takes her into a large dip.*]

[*Coming up from the dip. To the audience:*]

Jenny just went back to the table and kind of moved closer to my buddy's wife and got real quiet. Being so young and innocent, I figured she was awed by it all. She asked to go home early, and I took her back. I could feel the strong glare of the porch light her parents left on.

[*To* JENNY:]

Jenny, I'm a man who wants to know where he's at all the time. What's my altitude?

[*To the audience:*]

And she said: "Check your *attitude* not your altitude." She went in, slammed the door shut and snapped off the porch light.

[*A beat.*]

It was like being in thunderheads that you can't fly around or above. I walked back slowly to the car. I don't know why I turned on the radio. Maybe I needed to hear something besides my own heart pounding. Suddenly, H.V. Kaltenborn's voice was announcing that the Japanese had bombed Pearl Harbor.

[*A beat.*]

My God. We're at war!

[*To* JENNY. *He pounds on the seat of the chair.*]

Jenny! You got to come out! Right now! We're at war. The Japanese have bombed Pearl Harbor and they're headed straight for us. I have to take care of you, honey. I have to take care of your folks. And mine. And all of America.

[*To the audience:*]

That's the way we all felt when we heard about Pearl. I won't lie to you and say we weren't scared. Cause we were. Some people were glad. I know that's a strange thing to say. But the war suddenly shook all the loose pieces together in this country. We weren't drifting anymore. There was a unity now. War gave us a common cause, and that was exciting.

[*A beat.*]

Jenny and I were married one month later.

[*To* MUSEUM SPECTATOR:]

What was that? Am I still a "hawk?" What school do you

go to, kid? University of Denver? Well, Denver, we didn't have words like that in those days. I only knew of one conscientious objector during the whole war. They put him in the same detention camp in Oregon where that actor Lew Ayres was sent. Everybody wanted to get in on the fight. You'd see long lines in front of court houses and recruiting offices all across the country. There was a man in Moline who was nearly blind and even he joined up — memorized all the Army's eye charts and nearly made it through basic training. And don't forget Pearl Harbor! It was a massacre. Sunken ships, burned hangars, aircraft hulks everywhere. The ground was littered with body parts. The only way the Army could handle the dead was in a mass burial. American women were each given a grave number and a Hawaiian lei. That's all they had left of their husbands, their boyfriends, their sons. [*A beat.*] You young people today never had to sit through blackouts in your own living room not knowing if your home town would go up in flames.

[*To audience:*]

The Army was throwing every available kid at me. Farm boys who had their heads full of glory and John Wayne movies and nothing else.

I trained young pilots day after day. I had this one guy who flew over Florida and said: "That's not Florida — it ain't purple." Florida's purple on our official Army map. That's what I was dealing with...

[*To audience:*]

I'm not squeamish. Being a small town boy, I've helped our neighboring farmers birth a lot of cattle. Once I struggled inside a cow for hours trying to pull out her dead calf. Working up to my elbows like that — inside her — I never had to see the mother's eyes. But you come to terms with how you deal with death, especially if you're in the military. I believe a soldier like me is honorably anonymous. Or at least, that's the way it should be. My personal name doesn't matter. What do we know of the ordinary foot soldier in the Civil War or of the lonely infantryman in the trenches of W.W. I. I'm proud of being the pilot who dropped the bomb over Hiroshima, but I can hardly remember that man. I go to the library and see my name in the history books, and all I'm looking at is a couple of words strung together.

[*To the audience:*]

I'll tell you a secret about flying. I guess it's one of those "contradictions" of theory that Oppenheimer always liked to tell me about.

[*A beat.*]

All the wrong things make you a pilot. The wrong weather, the wrong take off, the wrong landing speed. We live by the mistakes that can kill us. Our task is to turn misfortune into dreams. Everybody and everything since the beginning of time: the Chinese, the Greeks. You see it carved on caves and walls — winged bulls, winged lions, men with wings strapped on them. Everybody wants the dream. The Wright Brothers — they were just tinkering. With 12 seconds...40 yards...they changed the world. What would those bicycle makers think now? Cause the sky is not a place where you can live. The atmosphere is just a trick. Every time I take off, I fly into something worse. All flight consists of feeling the astonishment of air after leaving the ordinary things of land.

[*A beat.*]

I first learned something secret and powerful might be going on after lunch with an old school buddy of mine, Curt. Cause at the University of Chicago where he was teaching, something about atoms was going on under the bleachers of old Stagg Field.

[*A beat.*]

That's the first time I ever heard of a chain reaction.

[*A beat.*]

Jenny was very pregnant about this time. We were both having trouble sleeping at night. I was worrying about the air-war getting bloodier in Europe. We'd drink lots of cocoa — cocoa wasn't rationed — and play Tommy Dorsey records.

[*To audience:*]

When Jimmy was born we gave him Orville for a middle name.

[*He cradles his infant son in his arms and talks to him:*]

Jimmy Orville, your daddy is going to ease out all the turbulence in your life.

[*He sings a lullaby to his infant son that is part "Air Force Song" and "All Through the Night."*]

[*Singing softly:*]

Off we go

into the wild blue yonder...

all through the night.

Pilot an-gels

God will lend thee,

all through the night.

Flying high

into the sun

love alone

my watch is keeping

all through the night.

[*To the audience:*]

Jenny couldn't buy diapers since all the cotton was going for bandages. That left cutting up some of my old white shirts. But before she had a chance to cut up *all* of them, I got orders to fly General Eisenhower to Africa. It was 1942.

[*A beat.*]

The day I met Ike to fly him out on a B-17, the weather was a solid wall of muck. Not a spot of reality anywhere. Ike was on his way to open the new front in North Africa.

[*He sits in the chair now piloting* IKE:]

    Sir. There's so much soup out there, even the birds are on foot.

[*To the audience:*]

    Silence.

[*To* IKE:]

    Sir. It's so thick out there, you can't even read the Burma Shave signs.

[*To the audience:*]

    Silence.

[*A beat.*]

    Suddenly, we skulked into some bright sunlight. The General relaxed and began chanting:

[IKE *chanting:*]

No German likes

the spacious sky

when our B-17's

happen by.

Burma Shave.

[*To the audience:*]

    And I answered the man who was to be President of the United States:

[*To* IKE:]

Into the sky

lickty-split!

It's a Messerschmitt

SPLAT

wasn't it.

Burma Shave.

Sir.

[*To the audience:*]

We laughed and ate Nabisco cookies Jenny had packed for us and Ike said to me:

[IKE *speaking:*]

Colonel, mom Eisenhower just made Mother of the Year in Kansas. Greatest award I ever received in my life. Better than making general.

[PILOT *speaking:*]

Sir...

[IKE *speaking:*]

It broke mother Eisenhower's heart when I went to West Point. She's a pacifist, you know.

[PILOT *speaking:*]

General Eisenhower, sir...

[IKE *speaking:*]

Over the years, I told her: Mom, don't be sorry, your son Ike is a pacifist lots of times.

[PILOT *speaking:*]

General Eisenhower, sir, we just got us an escort of ten American planes. We're about to land on African soil.

[*To the audience:*]

That was the last time I was ever to pilot the B-l7 as a chauffeur.

[*A beat.*]

I prepared Jenny for my new combat orders. Then I had to tell Mom.

[*To* MOM:]

Mom, will you sit down? I don't want any eggs. I just came

by to tell you...I got my combat orders. Probably at the end of this month. Germany. I just want you to know...I'm a good pilot. I learned self-reliance and bravery from you. Watching you pull a hot pie from the oven with your bare hands. [*A beat.*] Remember what that gypsy told you at the Mendota State Fair? That's right. Your son's never going to come to any harm in an airplane! [*Repeating to himself:*] I'm never going to come to any harm in an airplane.

[*He sits straight in the chair at the controls of his plane. To audience:*]

Combat! I was leading the formation in Red Gremlin with my favorite crew. Tailgunner, Cleve "Boo" Beckahazy, was a Bing Crosby fan and I could hear him singing as usual.

[TAILGUNNER *singing:*]

I can't take this tension boo boo boo...it's too much boo boo boo to mention. I can't boo boo boo ...

[*To* TAILGUNNER:]

Pilot to tailgunner. Over. You know another song? Out.

[TAILGUNNER *singing:*]

God boo boo boo bless A-mer-a-ca..boo boo boo ...

[*To the audience:*]

As Boo sang, the steady drone of the engines gave him some loud harmony.

[*To* TAILGUNNER:]

Pilot to tailgunner. Over. Cut the screeching, Boo. We're approaching Germany. Out.

[*To audience:*]

Three miles up sun, I could see the Messerschmitts. My wingman hadn't seen them. He was a kid of 20 right out of flight school. Now they were on us.

[*To* CREW:]

Break! Break! Enemy off the port wing, firing. After him...yah, we're closing in...that a way...fire! Fire! We torched him! He's rolling...showing belly...look, you can see the Black Cross on his tail.

[*To the audience:*]

Then I saw the canopy open and the German pilot hit the silk. His parachute floated right by our cockpit...so close I could see two little rivers of blood pouring from his mouth and down on his jacket. I'd done most of my military training banging away at shapeless black silhouettes on the rifle range. I never visualized my target as having eyes, nose and mouth. [*A beat.*] Suddenly the Kraut put one finger lengthwise under his nose in a Hitler mustache. His way of telling us that the Fuhrer was escaping. Wounded but alive. That's when I took my logbook pencil and held it out from my mouth like a cigarette holder — like victorious old Roosevelt. My crew cheered, but the Kraut didn't see me. He was falling gently and silently below us while his plane streamed black smoke and went straight to the ground, flaming.

[*To audience:*]

Sometimes after those aerial dog-fights, I'd have nightmares. Once, I dreamed a black horse was kicking the hell out of my machine.

[*To audience:*]

Nightmares have no meaning. They're senseless. Those things always go away, finally, if you don't make a big deal out of them.

[*A beat*]

I was called to Washington and then to Wendover on the Nevada border to begin my B-29 assignment. A test pilot and 10 technicians had just crashed in a B-29 test flight. The project was in chaos.

[*To crews:*]

I'm damn sick and tired of you guys griping about the B-29 and refusing to join her crews. [*A beat.*] So, I'll tell you what I'm going to do. I'm going to prove it to each and every one of you.

[*To the audience:*]

One day I just burst into the lounge of the women's barracks at Eglin AAFB in Florida.

[*To women in the barracks:*]

You WASPs have some four engine time? You...what's your name? De-De what? Johnson. Ok, Johnson, you say you're a radio control pilot? Good. I'm here to get two women to check out in the B-29. Interested? [*A beat.*] You're on. Me? Am I Charles Lindbergh? Sure, I'm Lindbergh. Who else? Dora Dougherty? ok? If you've been up in an A-20, a 1,600 horsepower twin-engine attack plane, that's good enough. Both of you be ready at 0600 tomorrow.

[*A beat.*]

I took De-De and Dora to Anniston, Alabama, and gave them a high powered concentrated three day briefing.

[*To the women on each side of him as he sits in the chair that becomes the plane. He lets* DE-DE *pilot the aircraft:*]

De-De, dear, now you need to taxi up to the runway quickly, then get it up. Cause, Babe, these engines sometimes explode if they go through regulated warm-up time. The 29 is a sweet tempermental female, so you're flying her woman to woman and you can think of that as an advantage. Ok...check above and behind to see if anybody's moving in our clearance. That's it, now...away we go. Easy. Skip the bumps and grinds and take it off! That's it...up...up ...yah. Good. [*A beat.*] Ok, now it's Dora's turn. Dora, sweetheart, let's practice some stalls at 3,000 feet.

[*He settles back comfortably, humming "I'll Be Seeing You." Suddenly, his head dives down near the floor and then sharply goes back up again. We can see that he is winded.*]

[*To* DORA:]

Dora, where the hell did you learn Hammerhead Stalls? You sure put some strain on the "29" [*Looking at controls.*]...but she's just fine.

[*To audience:*]

On May 20, 1943, a Superfortress B-29 now named *Ladybird* was approaching Tinker Field for the showdown. Crowds of men were gawking along the flight line. The whole crew of a B-17 was standing on top of the wings watching. I was on the ground watching, too. There for a few minutes, I felt lonely. That plane up there was my whole world, and now it was under the controls of two women. I was jealous.

[*Looking up at the women flying the B-29:*]

Ok, girls, do it right. Come on. [*A beat.*] Sure, I see you rocking your wings at me. [*He waves to their plane.*] That-a-way. Come on. Now enter the pattern. Easy. Easy. You're pulling a sweet greased on landing.

[*To audience:*]

The women climbed down from the bomber, took off their helmets and shook out their long hair. A navigator walked up to them and said: "Golly, you both are just little bitty things." De-De shot back: "It's only cause we're standing next to a 29 that's three stories tall."

[*A beat.*]

After that, I had no trouble signing up crews. But, unfortunately, Congressman John Rankin heard about my experiment and called the AAF Headquarters yelling: "Get those women out of my airplane." There was engine grease under their fingernails. When they did square loops and snap rolls, they were guys. But I couldn't use them.

[*A beat.*]

But shortly I had my own private Air Force and I was working 18 hours a day training crews. I didn't know I was really preparing for something called the A-Bomb.

[*A beat.*]

I met Dr. J. Robert Oppenheimer at a party one spring day in 1944. Both Oppenheimer and his wife, Kitty, were heavy drinkers and the early recruitment for the Manhattan Project was usually done over cocktails. You were asked to work with him on the war effort. That's all.

[*A beat.*]

When I first walked up to Oppenheimer, he handed me a martini and asked:

You know how to "free pour" a Martini without a shot glass, son?

Yes, Dr. Oppenheimer, I do know we're in a life and death struggle with the Germans and the Japanese. I'm drinking up…I'm drinking up. You most certainly can count on me to be a part of any effort that cuts this whole business short. Report where? 109 East Palace Avenue. In Sante Fe. [*He holds out the glass.*] A-one Martini.

[*To the audience:*]

First I was sent to a special top secret committee in the Pentagon. Two generals explained to me how I was to organize a combat force to carry a new bomb so powerful that nobody even knew what its exact force was. This bomb — estimated to be around 9,000 or 10,000 pounds — was presently being developed. The bomb bays of the B-29s under my command would have special modifications to take it on.

[*To the audience:*]

I made many visits to the City of Secrets in Lost Alamos where this pumpkin-shaped gimmick was being developed. It was part mountain resort and part scientific laboratory. Never in the history of the world had so many brilliant minds all come together in one place at one time. I'd leisurely walk around this shanty town of eggheads. The roads and foot paths were either mud holes or dust bowls. [*A beat.*] Nothing was ordinary in the Secret City. Infants were born with certificates listing place of birth as just Box 1663. Kids went to school with only first names. And everybody had a lot of college degrees.

[*To audience:*]

Late at night, I'd hear a piano. Oppenheimer was deflowering a new ditty he had composed, flooring the pedal. He could never sleep. [*A beat.*] And getting something to eat in the City of Secrets was always an event.

[*To customers in a sandwich shop:*]

This little shack serves hamburgers? Good. [*To waiter:*] I'll have a coke and burger. Well-done. Hold the onions. [*Looks to his fellow customers sitting beside him.*] How are the burgers here. Greasy? Sounds good. You guys always eat here? What did you say your names were? Fermi...Teller...Hans Bethe. Oh. Would you Laureates mind passing the catsup?

[*To the audience:*]

There was always excitement at Los Alamos. It was like a summer camp. People there all considered it an adventure since they were in a place that wasn't even supposed to exist. All mail and phone calls were censored. Visits to the outside were restricted to once a month. Residents were encouraged to cut off their families. The laboratory of the physicists on the hill was the true focal point although there were stores, movie houses and recreation centers all around it. There was also a 19 piece band, a choir, an orchestra and a radio station. The first year of its existence, out of a population of 6,000, one thousand babies were born.

[*To* OPPENHEIMER:]

Dr. Oppenheimer. You wanted to see me? I know you want me to wear civilian clothes when I come to Los Alamos. But, why? The scientists may be nervous about military men but just who do they think is going to drop their little "pumpkin?" They're quite willing to make it, but they don't like to think of it being used...not on people, anyway. Just how the hell are we going to pull that off? And while we're at it, those damn construction crews you got around here just dragged lumber through that stream by the lab. Now all the fish in there are dead cause you stirred up the mud. I was raised on a farm, Oppenheimer, and we don't do things like that to the land. And no, I will not stop wearing my uniform!

[*To audience:*]

I continued my vigorous training of the B-29 crews at Wendover and the Los Alamos crowd worked night and day on their gimmick. Then one morning, I got an urgent call from Oppenheimer. We met in a deserted hangar next to my office.

[*To* OPPENHEIMER:]

So, some of the scientists are getting cold feet? Don't they know Germany's working on some kind of bomb, too? A Laureate like yourself should lay down the law...oh, sorry...I didn't know you aren't a Nobel winner...no...no, it wasn't meant as a sarcastic slur. What's spooking everybody? Dr. Szilard found something disturbing? How disturbing? The gimmick could explode the air or the sea? In which case the earth would go...[*Snaps his fingers.*]. You said yourself that the calculations were safe. Congress is all for it. Truman just inherited the bomb? He sure as hell isn't interfering with us.

[*To the audience:*]

Oppenheimer did finally convince the others of his calculations, and work on the bomb continued and moved forward quickly. Now it was my job to find a way to deliver the gimmick without destroying my plane and crew.

[*A beat.*]

How to accurately drop this bomb and quickly pull away from the explosion? My worry was the weight of the bomb and the weight of the fuel for the 14 hour round trip flight. I decided to strip the "29" of all armament but the tail gun. That would save me 7,000 pounds. At 30,000 feet, we would be out of the range of any flak.

[*A beat.*]

I flew to Los Alamos to talk over my strategy with Oppenheimer. I landed at 0600, and he was waiting for me at the airstrip. It was chilly and he was holding out a steaming, welcoming cup of coffee.

[*To* OPPENHEIMER:]

Dr. Oppenheimer...how did you know I'd need coffee

right now more than anything in the world. [*He holds out his hand to take the coffee.*] *Coffee is coffee?* Yes, I sure agree with that. I'll just take it...the Hegelian philosophy says *this* cup of coffee is really beans? Sure...anything you say. But the Berkeleian holds that coffee only exists as dreams exists? Well, I'd really like some of that "dream" while it's hot. The Pragmatist says forget it's even coffee and only remember the stirring? No, I haven't read much Thomas Aquinas. He's a philosopher of common sense? Coffee is coffee? Right.

[*To the audience:*]

I finally got Oppenheimer away from Thomas Aquinas and on to the B-29. But my coffee was cold.

[*To* OPPENHEIMER:]

Okay, after the bomb hits, the minimum distance my plane can be safe is at 8 miles. The shock wave will come at me at about 1,000 feet a second...the speed of sound. I think the way for me to get away from the detonation is to do a quick turn of 155 degrees as soon as my bombardier lets go. Yes...yes...it does put a heavy strain on the "29". But she can take it. How do I know? A little lady named Dora whispered it in my ear.

[*A beat.*]

I realize that some of the scientists are spooked. But staging a demonstration of the bomb is out of the question. Drop it on a Japanese city after everybody's been evacuated? Are they crazy! The Japanese would take all their people out and put in every American prisoner of war they have. What about dropping it some deserted island? Show them our real power? What if it duds out on us! Then what? Those Japanese militarists would get worse. Who? Szilard sent a letter of protest to Truman? Who in the hell is Szilard? He first conceived the nuclear chain reaction? And now he's backing out? He's making a moral issue? A moral issue! When the Japanese are breathing down our necks. Let me see his letter. [*He takes the letter from* OPPENHEIMER *and reads it.*]

[*Reading* SZILARD'S *letter:*] "A nation which sets the precedent of using these newly liberated forces of nature for purposes of destruction may have to bear the responsibility of opening the door to an era of devastation on an unimaginable scale."

Leo Szilard

[*To* OPPENHEIMER:]

Why are people getting gun-shy all of a sudden, Dr. Oppenheimer? Well, I'm glad to know you're one-hundred-percent behind this project. What? Just because you're saying "yes" doesn't mean you really mean "yes." Since if you answer *no*, it wouldn't be a beginning but an end to the thousand steps of thought? Is this still *coffee is coffee?* Got you!

[*To* JENNY:]

I am not ignoring you, Jenny. You know what you're really mad about? Flying. Flying is leaving. Every time I go up, you feel I reject you. Honey, when I'm flying through the clouds, I'm not hot for anything beyond the skin of my plane. And if you can't accept that, this marriage won't last. And leave Jimmy out of this. My son and I do just fine.

[*To* JIMMY, *age three:*]

Jimmy Orville, we're planting a garden cause the President wants us to. Why? Cause everybody's got to help out. [*A beat.*] You got that bag of potatoes your mother gave us? Good. Take them out and pick off all the "eyes." Potato-eyes are seeds that will grow us more potatoes. That's right...put them in the holes. Now, next to this row of potato-eyes, we're going to plant carrot seeds. And next to the carrots — onions. The carrots are going to make the potato-eyes real strong, and the onions are going to make the potato-eyes water, and that way you and me don't have to stand out here and throw on fertilizer or run the hose all day long. [*A beat*] Remember, son, a garden is a wonderful thing. Saints have gardens. [*A beat.*] Now...what's that on your face?...Just a little dirt. Hey, you've got yourself a "victory face."

[*To* MUSEUM SPECTATORS:]

What did you say? How could I play with my little boy like that when I was getting ready to drop the bomb? I was thinking of Jimmy Orville and every American kid when I flew over Hiroshima. And for those guys sitting on ships waiting to invade Japan, too. I have never — for one moment — ever been sorry for what I did. On the contrary, I stopped the war!

[*He continues his story:*]

Final preparations began on Tinian. We won that island back from the Japanese, and now it was our Atomic launching pad. Sometimes we called Tinian — Manhattan. We named our streets Broadway...Forty-Second Street...Central Park West ...Riverside Drive...I had many long briefings with the Tinian Joint Chiefs on Park Avenue.

[*To the* TINIAN JOINT CHIEFS:]

Sirs. I don't think it's a good idea to send up the *Enola Gay* with a large escort and fly into Japan in formation. That will just alert their military. We can't afford to take any heavy duty anti-aircraft fire. Not with the pumpkin on board. [*A beat.*] I suggest we just kinda go in alone. Like we were a reconnaissance plane. [*A beat.*] My crew and I have my break-away maneuver well rehearsed. Heavy turbulence? Could that set off the bomb? The "pumpkin" can't be triggered unless there's a firing of an explosive inside it. What if the *Enola* cracks up during take off? Or catches fire? I've got that figured out, sirs. We make the final assembly of the bomb during flight. Can I do that? Hell, yes. We'll get us a good ordnance man to insert one of the uranium slugs and the explosive charge into the gimmick's casing when we're in the air. Sure, it'll be difficult in that cramped space. I'm not saying it's easy. But we'll do it.

[*To the audience:*]

The USS Indianapolis arrived off Tinian with the first Atomic Bomb. There was only one way we could load it. The bomb called "Little Boy" — covered in tarpaulin — had to be put into a hole in the ground. We taxied the plane over the top of hole — then jacked "Little Boy" right up into the *Enola's* belly...Our A-bomb was twelve feet long and 9,000 pounds.

[*A beat.*]

Three weather planes — *Straight Flush, Full House, Jabbitt III* — were to precede me by one hour and fly over the primary and secondary targets. *The Great Artiste* would follow and drop instruments by parachute to record the blast and measure radio activity.

[*A beat*]

August 6, 12:30 a.m. 1945. We of the 509th Composite Group picked up our gear and headed for the airstrip. We were designated Special Bombing Mission #13. None of us were superstitious about that. Hell, the bad luck of "13" was for the other guys. When we got to the flight line, the *Enola Gay* was lustrous with all the spot-lights shining on her. The Press was everywhere. *Enola* was like a movie star at a world premiere. I had come a long way from that little town in Illinois where mom ironed a newspaper for my kites.

[*To a* MUSEUM SPECTATOR:]

I don't know why so many Americans treat me like I'm Frankenstein or something. The Japanese never do that. When I went to Asia after the war, those people didn't run away from me, screaming. In a way, they respect me more than most of you do. I see Japanese folks here in the States; they don't consider me any big deal. I'm just somebody who did his job. That's all. [*A beat.*] Isn't that a Japanese woman over there? Yah, sure it is. [*He takes a piece of paper out of his shirt pocket. He mimes making it into a paper plane.*] Little lady, come closer. Where you from? Won't you look up at me? [*He makes as if to sail the paper plane in the air. He then hands her the plane.*] Just a plane with silent wings. Come on, don't be shy. [*A beat as she hands him something, her face still downward.*] What are you giving me? [*He takes a paper crane from her.*] A crane? [*He pulls the crane apart like an accordion and many paper cranes unfold.*] So many cranes. For me? [*A beat.*] Won't you give me a smile, little mama-san? [*A beat as he watches her slowly lift her face to him. He slowly backs away from her.*] Oh, God! What happened to you! What's wrong with your face? God! [*He throws the cranes down on the floor.*] Who told you to do this? Who put you up to this? I didn't do that to your face? Stay away from me. Stay away! All I did was stop a war. I don't regret anything!

[*He kicks the cranes away from him as if they were alive. He turns his back to the audience. After a beat, we see him stoop over at the waist, slowly. After a pause, we hear him talk into the plane's interphone softly, still stooped with his back turned:*]

[*To the crew of the Enola Gay:*]

Men, years from now, the citizens of our great country will be watching a movie about what we do today. So...no cussing. No spitting. No scratching. Remain calm but alert.

[*He stands and turns to the audience and faces his crew.*]

I'll be passing out special goggles to each crew member before take-off. Have them ready to use when I give the order. [*A beat.*] Now, let's go have a good breakfast before we move out.

[*To the audience:*]

August 5. 1 a.m. Mess sergeant, Elliott Easterly, had decorated the quonset-mess with cardboard pumpkins. We all took one off the wall for a good luck charm.

[*A beat.*]

2 a.m. Our weather planes had already left. Eleven crew members entered the B-29 ahead of me. I was ready to hop on when Dr. Don Young pulled me aside.

[*To DR. YOUNG:*]

Whaddya got for me, Doc? 12 cyanide pills? One for each of us? No pain with these, huh? You're right...something goes wrong, I sure as hell don't wanna hit the silk. Guys I've known who got captured by the Japanese were tortured pretty bad. Especially after the fire-bombings in Tokyo. I know...I know...this isn't easy for you. But Doc, I'm planning on success. We just got a big send-off prayer from the Chaplain. We'll do the job. You'll see.

[*To the audience:*]

On board, I settled into the left seat. Bob Lewis was my co-pilot. We had crew from all around the U.S. — New Mexico, Nevada, Texas, New Jersey, North Carolina, New York, Pennsylvania, Maryland, Michigan, California, and *my* states, Iowa and Illinois.

[*Speaking from the captain's seat of the Enola Gay:*]

Crew, synchronize watches. 0230.

[*A beat.*]

Auxiliary power turned on. [*A beat.*] Electrical system — check. Start up engines. [*A beat.*] All engines go. [*A beat.*] Oil pressure — check. Fuel pressure — check. Brakes set —check.

[*A beat.*]

Remove the wheel chocks. [*A beat.*] *Great Artiste* behind us — Roger. Ready to taxi out. [*He puts both thumbs up.*]

[*To the audience:*]

Every take-off is different. It's a crucial time. But now it was important beyond anything I had ever done before. With 7,000 gallons of gas and a 9,000 pound atomic bomb, we were loaded well beyond normal capacity. I was determined to remain calm. After all, hadn't I taken off hundreds of times before? I pretended I was with old Earl Ebberly and we were winging our way to Bettendorf, Iowa, to drop candy.

[*To the tower:*]

Redbird six three to North Tinian Tower. Ready for take-off on Runway Able. [*A beat.*] Cleared for takeoff. Roger.

[*To CREW:*]

Release breaks. [*A beat.*] We're rolling now...two miles of runway and we're just gonna take it slow...we're doing 50 miles an hour...70 miles an hour...90...120...end of runway approaching...I'm holding her for 10 more miles an hour...I need all the power I can get for lift off. Hold tight...hang on...we're just about there...ahhhhhh...and up...at 140 miles per hour.

Nice and smooth. [*A beat.*] Take off time — 0245. Cameras roll.

[*To the audience:*]

Eight minutes airborne, and Parsons began to plug the uranium into the core of "Little Boy." [*A beat.*] Behind us was *Top Secret*, the airplane that would follow us all the way to Iwo Jima in case the *Enola* had some kind of mechanical problem and we needed a spare plane.

[*To* CREW *on interphone:*]

Hey, you guys in isolation, I'm coming back there for a little visit. Yah, I know I gotta crawl 30 feet through a stinking tunnel that's only 20 inches wide. I don't have the belly on me like some of you boozers. I can make it in nothing flat.

[*He takes off his shirt and his shoes and socks and crawls back to them. He is in his undershirt, trousers, and barefoot.*]

Coming through...coming through. What did I tell you? Slipped right through. [*A beat.*] Nice place you got here. Who's got the hot chocolate? How about hitting me with a cup. Thanks. [*He drinks.*] You guys wanna guess what we have on board? You know it's gotta be important if we were served *real* eggs not powdered for chow. Hey, don't be afraid to speak up. All security's off. This is it. The secret's going to be out pretty damn quick. [*A beat.*] Well, I'll just have to tell you. We're carrying the first Atomic Bomb. Yah! How about that! No kidding. You'll be able to see this bomb from anywhere. Even Paw Paw, Illinois, will see this one. So...what are you guys thinking about right now? Sitting here beside the world's first A-incendiary? [*A beat.*] Buttermilk pancakes! That's what you're thinking about on the most important day of your life? I'll tell you what I'm thinking about. I'm thinking of the word "atom." How it's not going to be a secret or a mystery anymore. One of the scientists — Oppenheimer explained that a philosopher named Spinoza said a stone falling could think: "I want to fall." I figure that bomb knows it wants to fall, too.

[*He crawls back to the captain's seat.*]

Altitude 15,000 feet. Wind from the south. [*On interphone:*]

Pilot to navigator, keep me posted on any changes in radar wind runs. Over.

[*To* CO-PILOT:]

Bob, I think I'll just take a little cat nap. Look after the automatic pilot. And wake me up when we're ready to begin our climb over Iwo Jima.

[*To the audience:*]

I don't think I really slept. At a time like that, your past comes at you in crazy little flashes. The smell of lemon oil furniture polish mom used on holidays. The wallpaper of fading cabbage roses in the parlor. Of course I couldn't get old man Ebberly out of my mind and how he always said I had to "watch the ground." And...I thought about that last time I saw Oppie. Yah, I sometimes called Oppenheimer that like all his science buddies. I think he got to like me cause the first thing I said everytime I saw him was — *coffee is coffee.* Not that I ever really understood what the hell that meant. I figure it was like our guys saying "on a wing and a prayer." Anyway, Oppie came to Tinian that day we loaded "Little Boy" on the *Enola.* He watched the whole thing in silence and with a very sad face. His depression shocked me. This was supposed to be the high point of all his hard work. But all he could think about was how the bomb would throw us back into the crude stone age of reason. Because now theory had lost its core. In the final analysis, we should *not* understand. Science is fantasy. For an equation to be true, Oppie reasoned, it was necessary that at least on one level it had to be false. That is why physics was an art. Contradictions. "Little Boy" eliminated what couldn't be solved. There was nothing left for him anymore.

[*A beat.*]

Oppenheimer's words wouldn't get out of my head. In some strange way I felt implicated in his depression. But I couldn't understand why. I was doing what he wanted me to do. I was doing what they all wanted me to do...the scientists, Truman...Stimson...Congress...the dead at Pearl if they could speak for themselves.

[*A beat.*]

It was just beginning to get light. I broke open a little pack of Zinnia seeds Mom gave me and tossed them under my seat for luck. Everything was smooth and steady. When we came to Iwo Jima, I took the controls. Our standby plane swerved away from us and landed.

[*A beat.*]

We were now three hours away from our possible targets —either Hiroshima, Kokura or Nagasaki. We were proceeding smoothly, waiting anxiously for instructions from the three weather plane. What would be our target? Oppenheimer said Hiroshima was the best because it had flat terrain that would allow the bomb to "run out." I climbed to 30,700 feet, our bombing altitude. Orders were for a visual drop only. No radar sighting. If we suddenly got bad weather, we were to return to Tinian with Parsons disarming the bomb on the way home.

[*A beat.*]

People always want to know what I was thinking when I was only moments away from dropping the first A-Bomb. What were my deepest, innermost thoughts? It's hard to remember. In a sense, that man is an illusion to me. He is many illusions. Looking back, which one do I remember? I don't wish to change the thoughts of somebody who is no longer here to defend himself. After all, who I am *now* is not that pilot who has disappeared into history. I was probably thinking about the flights of W W. I, and how opposing pilots could lean out of their wood-and-rag planes and fire revolvers at each other. A flying surface was once as human as the flying carpet of the Arabian Nights. Now everything is precision and electronic navigation.[*A beat.*] When the target was in range, it was procedure at that time for the pilot to remove his hands from the controls and turn the ship over to the bombadier. Technically, I wasn't even at the helm when the pneumatic bomb-bay doors opened and "Little Boy" dropped. I felt cheated. The only human experience was the explosion and the victims. The days of Earl Ebberly and *The Wilma* when a man hunched down inside the cockpit and let the plane get inside of him were long gone. Now, a pilot simply stepped up and climbs inside the plane. Spots used to talk about his farmer friend, Sig Mosley, who got up one morning and drove his tractor all the way to the coast, then pushed that tractor into the ocean. Said he wanted things to get back to the way they were.

[*Into radio:*]

   Straight Flush. Come in. This is *Enola Gay*. [*A beat.*] Y-3, B-2, C-l. Code received. Roger and out.

[*A beat.*]

   Attention crew. [*A beat.*] The name of our target has just been transmitted from *Straight Flush*. [*A beat.*] It's…Hiroshima!

[*On interphone:*] Pilot to Bombardier. What is the status of "Little Boy?" Bomb is alive. Roger.

[*To crew:*]

   The city is coming into view. Be prepared for Initial Point, 15 miles east of target. Sighted — eight large ships in the harbor below. No flak visible.

[*A beat.*]

   We are approaching our primary. Secure your goggles on your forehead and prepare to use them at bomb release. Do not look into the flash.[*A beat.*] All crew, if you agree, please verify by saying after me: "This…is Hiroshima." [*A beat.*] Hiroshima. Check. [*A beat.*] 9:15 and 17 seconds. Hiroshima time: 8:15 and 17 seconds. [*A beat.*] Bombardiere, take over the aircraft. [*He holds up his hands away from the controls and moves back in his chair. A beat.*] Bomb-bay doors opening. "Little Boy"…falling. [*After a brief pause, he takes over the controls again.*] Prepare for break-away dive!

[*Now stripped to his trousers and [sleeveless] khaki-undershirt and bare feet, He holds up the chair and turns it sharply to the right in the break-away dive.*]

[*He speaks the following monologue while he holds the plane in the break-away dive:*]

A mushroom foams up at me in a churling mass of spiking mauve gray. Buds of raw green illuminate on every side. The earth's history blooms and exaggerates itself into the atmosphere: Stalks of lamp black and coal tar, stems of sienna, plants of brittle skin gold…shimmering-black leaves…yellow arsenic blossoms. I hear Oppie quoting Montaigne: "And if you have lived one day, you have seen everything. One day is equal to all days. There is no other light, there is no other darkness. The whole disposition of the heavens is the same." Now Montaigne is wrong. It's Oppenheimer's science rotting to the knowable. Today will never be like another day. I have made another light. I have made another darkness. I've changed the Heavens. [*He now begins shaking from the plane's turbulance.*] A fierce boiling red orb, five miles wide, rages towards me at a hundred million degrees. I throw the sun!

Rich Orloff

OEDI

Rich Orloff

Rich Orloff is an award-winning, unknown playwright. His full-length plays include the comedies *Damaged Goods* (winner, 1994 Playwrights First Award), *Veronica's Position* (winner, 1995 New Plays in America Festival), *Water Boy* (winner, 1997 InterPlay International Play Festival), *Someone's Knocking*, and *Domestic Tranquility* (finalist, 1998 McLaren Comedy Playwriting Competition). He also wrote the drama *Days of Possibilities*, adapted from true stories of college life during the Vietnam era. Rich's plays have been seen at such regional theaters as American Stage Company in New Jersey, Arizona Theatre Company, Florida Studio Theatre, and the Key West Theatre Festival.

His many one-act comedies include *The Whole Shebang* which was published in *The Best American Short Plays 1994-95*, and *I Didn't Know You Could Cook* which was published in *The Best American Short Plays 1996-97*. His short play *August Afternoon* was recently published in *Ten-Minute Plays from Actors Theatre of Louisville, Volume Four*.

Oedi and *I Didn't Know You Could Cook* were originally produced by the Carousel Theatre Company as part of a trio of Rich's one-acts entitled *Sexy People*. *Oedi* was directed by Jonathan Alan Arak and performed by Steven Satta, Susan Grace, Scott Barrow, Mark Wellen, and Sundra Jean Williams.

Rich lives in New York City with his wife Amy and several sturdy plants.

CHARACTERS:

OEDIPUS, King of Thebes, early thirties

TIRESIAS, a blind, old seer

CREON, Oedipus' advisor and brother-in-law

JOCOSTA, Oedipus' wife, among other things

THE TOWN CRIER, heard off-stage

Ancient Greece. Around 4 p.m.

A room in the palace of OEDIPUS *the king, simply furnished. A chair and perhaps a column or two. The chair should be in the style of ancient Greece, without backs. In the distance, we hear the call of the* TOWN CRIER.

TOWN CRIER: [*Off-stage.*] Hear ye, hear ye! Four o'clock and all is well. Details at eleven. For the best in dining delicacies, treat yourself to Hecuba's House of Hummus! Try their babago-noosh!...Plato says, "It's ideal!"

[TIRESIAS *and* CREON *enter.* TIRESIAS *is blind and uses a cane.*]

CREON: Oedipus!

OEDIPUS: Creon, my trusted aide; Tiresias, noble seer. At last you have returned! My mind has been able to dwell on nothing save what news you may have found on your journey.

TIRESIAS: If it is good news for which you wait, you wait in vain. I see nothing but gloom and doom!

OEDIPUS: Creon, is that true?

CREON: Oedipus, my dear brother-in-law, perhaps we should hold off telling you anything until we have gathered all of our information.

OEDIPUS: I cannot wait. Ever since the plague has hit our beloved Thebes, the people insist that we find the killer of their former king, as they are convinced that until we punish the murderer, the plague shall continue. As their new king, I owe them the truth as quickly as possible. Besides, the latest polls show my popularity's plummeting.

CREON: Yes, but —

OEDIPUS: There is no time for "but"s. I created the Creon Commission to ferret out the facts of this fearsome felony, and I demand to know what you have learned.

CREON: Well, first we visited the oracles of Delphi to see what they could tell us.

OEDIPUS: Were the oracles helpful?

TIRESIAS: Well, you know oracles. It's hard to get a straight answer out of them.

CREON: They did tell us that old king Laios was murdered by his own son.

OEDIPUS: But that's crazy. Laios had no son.

CREON: Actually, we discovered he did, many years ago, but the child was banished as an infant. People assumed the child died in the wilderness.

OEDIPUS: Poor child. I feel his pain, as if it were my own.

TIRESIAS: Funny you should say that.

CREON: We did some checking, and learned the child had been rescued by a shepherd.

OEDIPUS: Oh, good.

CREON: And the child grew up to be about your height, your weight, and according to descriptions, he looked a lot like you.

OEDIPUS: What a coincidence.

CREON: Oedipus, how to put this...You know how much I admire you. When you first came to town, it was I who encouraged the people to make you king. And as you know, well, before we made you king, well, we never did a lot of checking into your background.

OEDIPUS: I have led a completely pious life.

CREON: I'm sure it's been very pious, but, well, in between those many, many years of piety, you never murdered anyone, did you?

OEDIPUS: I want to state unequivocally that I have never murdered anyone, depending on a very strict legal definition of murder.

CREON: Did you, say, kill anyone on your journey here?

OEDIPUS: Let me recall my journey. I decided it was time to leave Corinth and seek my fortune in the world. So I decided to journey to Thebes. I stopped off for a visit with the poet Sappho, who I used to think had a crush on me but now I have my doubts, and then I continued on the Thebes Highway. When I got to the town of Phokis, I met a hostile band of travellers. One of them said something obnoxious to me, so I clubbed them all to death. Other than that, I didn't kill anyone.

TIRESIAS: What'd the man say that was so obnoxious?

OEDIPUS: He called me a mama's boy.

TIRESIAS: For that you clubbed him to death?

OEDIPUS: What can I say? He got my goat, and I liked my goat very much.

CREON: Well, Oedipus, I don't know how to tell you this, but we learned that Laios was clubbed to death in the town of Phokis. And everyone in his party was killed before they got out of Phokis.

OEDIPUS: You're not suggesting I — I'd never kill a king. It's — It's inappropriate.

CREON: But he was on a religious pilgrimage.

OEDIPUS: You mean —

TIRESIAS: He always dressed down for those things.

OEDIPUS: Then it's possible I…I…

TIRESIAS: If the sandal fits.

OEDIPUS: But Tiresias, you prophesied that Laios would be killed by his own son. I never even met the man before.

[CREON *and* TIRESIAS *say nothing.*]

OEDIPUS: [*Cont'd.*] This is going to be a real bad news day, isn't it?

CREON: Oedipus, we discovered Polybus and Merope weren't your real parents. You're an orphan.

OEDIPUS: Wow, this is a lot to deal with.

TIRESIAS: We also know that the son of Laios had a birthmark in the shape of an olive on the bottom of his left foot.

[CREON *stares at* OEDIPUS' *left foot.*]

OEDIPUS: Well, we'll just have to search all of Greece until we find out where that child is. Let's start at the end of the kingdom and work our way back.

CREON: I think we must start here.

OEDIPUS: But I hate taking off my sandals. It always takes so long to lace them back up.

CREON: The people will be furious unless you can prove your innocence.

OEDIPUS: You really think they'll be angry?

TIRESIAS: Is the earth flat?

[OEDIPUS *unlaces his left sandal and lifts his left foot. On the bottom of his foot is a birthmark in the shape of a huge green olive with a red pimento.*]

OEDIPUS: As you can see, my foot has no such mark.

CREON: It looks like an olive to me.

OEDIPUS: Tiresias?

TIRESIAS: I see nothing.

OEDIPUS: I'll go with Tiresias.

CREON: Oedi, admit it. That's an olive.

OEDIPUS: I prefer to think of it as an unripe eggplant with ketchup on it.

CREON: It's an olive.

OEDIPUS: Okay, okay. Technically speaking, it's an olive. I must be the son of Laios, and I've killed my own father in a rage! I did a very bad thing. Now can we drop it?

CREON: I'm sorry, my lord, but given your public statements on the matter, I'm afraid I can't.

OEDIPUS: Oh, woe to me and those who dwell in my house! I've slain a king, and I promised the people I'd put the killer to death. I even said "Read my lips." But wait! One thing isn't clear.

TIRESIAS: Here comes the messy part.

OEDIPUS: If I'm Laios' son, and if Laios was married to Jocasta, who is now my wife, that means, that means, that means — Laios must've had a previous wife, right?

CREON: I'm afraid not.

OEDIPUS: Did he ever fool around on the side?

CREON: Never.

OEDIPUS: Sperm donor?

CREON: Nope.

OEDIPUS: Are you saying my wife is also my, my ...

TIRESIAS: Bullseye!

OEDIPUS: Oh my gods! Oh my gods! I've married my mother!! No wonder she always knows what I want for breakfast. Oh my gods! I've murdered my father and married my mother!

TIRESIAS: It could be worse. You could've murdered your mother and married your father. Then you'd be in real trouble.

OEDIPUS: Who else knows?

CREON: Don't worry. Only the staff of the Creon Commission, all of whom are completely trustworthy.

[*We hear:*]

TOWN CRIER: [*O.S.*] Hear ye, hear ye! The King is shtupping his mother, details at 11!

OEDIPUS: Oh, wretched day! Oh, cursed life! How can I expunge the evil deed from my soul? There is only one way! I must pluck out my eyes immediately!

[OEDIPUS *tries to pluck out his eyes, but* CREON *holds his arms back.*]

CREON: Don't do it!

OEDIPUS: Let go of me!

TIRESIAS: Don't do it! You'll have a moment's satisfaction, and a lifetime of wondering if your toga's on straight.

OEDIPUS: Okay, okay. Let go...Does my beloved wife know about this?

CREON: Not yet.

OEDIPUS: Oh, how can I break this news to her? How can I tell her without breaking her heart? Her face is too lovely for tears. Her soul is too pure for grief.

[*We hear:*]

JOCASTA: [*O.S.*] Yoo-hoo, oh, Oedi!

CREON: The queen approaches.

OEDIPUS: [*Calling out.*] In here, snookums!

[JOCASTA *enters. She's easily thirty or more years older than* OEDIPUS. *If she happens to be short and speaks with a slight old world inflection, so much the better.*]

JOCASTA: Oedileh, I was wondering if — Oh, am I disturbing something?

[*Simultaneously:*]

OEDIPUS:	CREON:
Yes!	No. We were just leaving.
	Right, Tiresias?

TIRESIAS: Oh, right. It's time for me to practice my musical instrument.

JOCASTA: Lyre?

TIRESIAS: No, honestly.

[CREON *and* TIRESIAS *exit.*]

JOCASTA: I didn't know you were in a meeting.

OEDIPUS: It was the most important meeting of my life.

JOCASTA: More important than when we met and you became my blintz of bliss?

OEDIPUS: Jocasta, I must tell you something most horrible, worse than the most terrible news you could imagine.

JOCASTA: You didn't like my brisket last night?

OEDIPUS: That's not it.

JOCASTA: What a relief. I was afraid I used too many bay leaves.

OEDIPUS: Oh, I cannot bear to tell you.

JOCASTA: My toga's too short, isn't it? You think a woman my age —

OEDIPUS: Your toga's fine.

JOCASTA: Are we having problems I'm unaware of in the horizontal department?

OEDIPUS: No, everything's fine in the — Jocasta, I just received the preliminary report of the Creon Commission.

JOCASTA: Oh, good. As soon as we name the murderer of Laios and make him drink some seltzer with a shpritz of hemlock, I know your approval rating will bounce right back.

OEDIPUS: I don't think so.

JOCASTA: Why not?

OEDIPUS: Jocasta, my beloved ...

JOCASTA: Oedipus, my Corinthian column of love ...

OEDIPUS: Jocasta...The murderer of your late husband stands before you.

JOCASTA: You killed Laios?

OEDIPUS: Yes.

JOCASTA: Oh, no! Horror of horrors! I suddenly feel like plucking —

OEDIPUS: Don't pluck your eyes out!

JOCASTA: No, I feel like plucking a chicken. I'm so stressed. How are we going to put a spin on this so the public doesn't hate you?

OEDIPUS: Don't you hate me?

JOCASTA: Nah.

OEDIPUS: But I murdered your first husband!

JOCASTA: How can I hate you for something I thought of doing every single day of our marriage?

OEDIPUS: I thought you loved him.

JOCASTA: Feh.

OEDIPUS: You didn't love him?

JOCASTA: What's to love? The man snored, he had bad breath, and when I think of the things that man made me do ...

OEDIPUS: You mean, in the bedroom?

JOCASTA: Worse, in the kitchen. I'd make him a nice roast chicken, and he'd make me melt some feta cheese on it. The man had no class.

OEDIPUS: But when I first met you, you were in deep mourning.

JOCASTA: My press people insisted. I wanted to go sunbathing on Crete.

OEDIPUS: I didn't know.

JOCASTA: So you see, my darling, the news is not that bad at all.

OEDIPUS: But I have not told you all of it, and the news that remains is so horrendous my lips can barely form the shapes to say the misbegotten words.

JOCASTA: Can it wait? In fifteen minutes, I have my belly dancer-cize class.

OEDIPUS: Jocasta, do you remember the prophecy of Tiresias that your husband would be murdered by your son?

JOCASTA: Yes, also remember he prophesied...*The Iliad* would never make it as a novel.

OEDIPUS: Jocasta, I...I cannot tell you. The shame is too deep.

JOCASTA: Don't feel ashamed, my beloved.

OEDIPUS: Please say no more. Your words of affection only make it more difficult.

JOCASTA: Why?

OEDIPUS: Because...Because there's reason to believe that, by some ferocious folly of the fates, you married your own son.

JOCASTA: So?

OEDIPUS: Did you not hear me? I'm your son!

JOCASTA: So tell me something I don't know.

OEDIPUS: You know I'm your son?

JOCASTA: From the first moment you came into town. I took one look at those eyes, that smile, that — oh, wait a second, you have a little shmutz on your forehead.

[JOCASTA *licks her fingers and begins to wipe* OEDI'S *forehead.*]

OEDIPUS: Stop that!

JOCASTA: I just want you should look presentable.

OEDIPUS: How could you know I was your son and not tell me?

JOCASTA: I didn't think it was significant.

OEDIPUS: You married me!

JOCASTA: You asked.

OEDIPUS: I know, but —

JOCASTA: I would've been happy just dating; you were the one in a hurry. "Marry me, Jocasta, and I'll be the happiest man on earth." What mother could refuse such an offer?

OEDIPUS: But I killed Dad!

JOCASTA: So? He never liked you anyway.

OEDIPUS: He didn't?

JOCASTA: Once he heard Tiresias' prediction that you were destined to murder him, he insisted you be sent away. I said, "Can't we wait and see? Maybe he'll just wound you a little."

OEDIPUS: This is the most devastating day of my life.

JOCASTA: Look, you're here and all is well, so unless there's some more news, I want to get to my belly dancercize class. Next week we start navel exercises, so I need to be in ship shape.

OEDIPUS: Don't you think we have some issues to discuss?

JOCASTA: Like what?

OEDIPUS: Like the fact that we can no longer live as husband and wife.

JOCASTA: Why not?

OEDIPUS: Because you're my mother!

JOCASTA: You say that like it's a negative.

OEDIPUS: Men cannot marry their mothers!

JOCASTA: None of my friends feel that way.

OEDIPUS: But —

JOCASTA: From what I've heard, most men marry women who remind them of their mothers. So I figure why settle for second best when you can have the real thing?

OEDIPUS: But I can't have sex with you knowing you're my mother.

JOCASTA: Not even on weekends?

OEDIPUS: No!

JOCASTA: I bet you want to do it with Helen, that Trojan slut, don't you?

OEDIPUS: No.

JOCASTA: Then who do you want to do it with?

OEDIPUS: I want to be with a woman to whom I'm not already related.

JOCASTA: I see. So now the whole family's not good enough to have sex with.

OEDIPUS: Will you be reasonable?! I'm a public official. I'm a role model.

JOCASTA: So? Look at the Gods. The immortal Zeus has slept with his half-sister, his quarter-sister, his sixteenth- sister. If our own immortal gods get to boff their relatives, why can't you?

OEDIPUS: Because you're not just a relative, you're my mother!

JOCASTA: Must you make everything so complex, Oedipus?...[*If the audience moans,...she addresses them:*] Hey, it's better than the navel joke, so be grateful.

OEDIPUS: Jocasta, this abomination against nature cannot continue.

JOCASTA: Look, Oedileh, I understand this is traumatic for you. But in a healthy marriage, you work through these things.

OEDIPUS: We don't have a healthy marriage!

JOCASTA: You want we should see a counselor?

OEDIPUS: No!

JOCASTA: Then what are you saying?

OEDIPUS: Mom...I want a divorce.

[JOCASTA *breaks into hysterical crying.*]

JOCASTA: I never thought I'd hear such a thing from my own son.

OEDIPUS: Oh, wretched day, oh monstrous doom. And I'm sure when Sophocles hears about this, he'll try to turn it into another one of his lurid docudramas.

JOCASTA: Listen, sweetheart, don't split up something wonderful.

OEDIPUS: But I must do something so the people...will forgive my unfortunate foray into forbidden familial fornication.

JOCASTA: Call in your advisors. See what they say.

OEDIPUS: [*Calling out:*] Get me Creon and Tiresias!

[CREON *and* TIRESIAS *enter.*]

CREON: Yes, my lord?

OEDIPUS: That was fast.

TIRESIAS: Well, um, uh, we remembered I left something in your outer office, and —

OEDIPUS: Have you two been spying on me?

CREON: We have dedicated our hearts and souls to you. How could you accuse us of such a monstrosity?

[*We hear:*]

TOWN CRIER [*O.S.*]: Hear ye! Hear ye! Jocasta refuses to grant Oedipus a divorce! Details at 11, followed by a special report and a half-hour of wisecracks by the village idiot.

TIRESIAS: First thing in the morning, I promise to find the source of these leaks.

OEDIPUS: [*Temper rising.*] If I find out either of you —

CREON: I have been busy, my lord, making some initial inquiries into public response to the crisis.

OEDIPUS: And what have you learned?

CREON: The people are confused. 85% of those polled strongly agreed with the statement, "If two people love each other, nothing else in a marriage is important."

JOCASTA: Aha!

CREON: But 54% also believe that those who commit incest should be boiled alive in non-virgin olive oil.

OEDIPUS: Of course, if I didn't know she was my mother, does it still fit the technical legal definition of incest?

CREON: Oedipus, get real.

OEDIPUS: And give up a life in politics? Never.

TIRESIAS: Why don't you start a war? That's always a good distraction.

OEDIPUS: I'm not going to start a war just to boost my approval rating.

TIRESIAS: How about a major rescue mission?

OEDIPUS: No! Oh, what can I do?

CREON: Well, from my polling, I definitely think that divorce would be unwise. To separate at a time of personal crisis would lose the family vote.

JOCASTA: Oh, what a happy day this is! Let the ouzo pour!

CREON: But we still don't have a solution to the crisis.

OEDIPUS: As far as I'm concerned, there's only one answer which will prove to the people I show my remorse for my sins.

TIRESIAS: You don't mean —

OEDIPUS: I must pluck out my eyes!

JOCASTA: You do that; don't expect me to lead you to the bathroom in the middle of the night.

OEDIPUS: I must do it! It's my only chance to earn the forgiveness of my people.

JOCASTA: Wouldn't a sincere "I'm sorry" suffice?

OEDIPUS: No! Give me your golden pins.

[OEDI *grabs two large pins from* JOCASTA'S *toga or hair.*]

CREON: Oedipus, don't!

OEDIPUS: Don't try to stop me, I warn you!

TIRESIAS: You fool!

OEDIPUS: Get away, or I'll punish you for trying to stop me!

TIRESIAS: What are you going to do, make me deaf?

OEDIPUS: Silence! Stand back!

[*Raising the pins.*]

I declare myself guilty of wretchedness and sin! From this hour forth, I go in darkness!

[OEDIPUS *is about to plunge the pins into his eyes, but he stops at the last moment.*]

OEDIPUS [*Cont'd.*] Or: Maybe I'll just cut off the offending organ which caused the sinful deed. That's it! I'll save my sight, but lose my jewels.

JOCASTA: Oedipus, no!!

OEDIPUS: I declare myself guilty of wretchedness and sin! From this hour forth, I go in eunuchness!

[OEDIPUS *is about to plunge the pins into his pelvic region, but stops at the last moment.*]

OEDIPUS: [*Cont'd.*] Or: Maybe I'll just cut off my arm. It's a more visible symbol anyway. People will never know if I've really castrated myself, but if I cut off my arm, my left arm, or maybe just one of my fingers, since we're talking symbolic action, anyway!

JOCASTA: Maybe you could just give some money to charity.

TIRESIAS: Maybe if you bit your lip and cried in public.

OEDIPUS: I give up.

CREON: You know, Oedipus, the more I think about it, the more I wonder, why are we driving ourselves into such a tizzy? You know how fickle the people are. Today they'll want to burn you at the stake; in a week, they'll be obsessed with the latest gossip about the gods.

OEDIPUS: But —

CREON: All we need is one good speech and a heartfelt explanation.

OEDIPUS: But how can we explain such a monstrous deed?

CREON: Well, it's not like you married your mother on purpose.

JOCASTA: Oh, no, he'd be too embarrassed to do that.

OEDIPUS: Jocasta!

TIRESIAS: I see the future!

OEDIPUS: What do you see?

TIRESIAS: The Olympics will never catch on.

OEDIPUS: Oh, what am I to do? If only the gods would give me a sign.

CREON: Maybe they have.

OEDIPUS: They have?

CREON: Run with me a little. Tiresias saw your fate when you were born; you tried your best not to live it out, but there are powers beyond those of we poor mortals.

OEDIPUS: I get it! Any efforts to forswear malfeasance were futile; it was the fault of the fates!

CREON: Exactly.

OEDIPUS: I'll make a speech where I'll take complete responsibility for my actions, but none of the blame.

TIRESIAS: Now that's good political thinking.

CREON: We'll say you wanted to smote out your eyes, but you placed your sense of public duty ahead of your own desires.

OEDIPUS: That's good.

TIRESIAS: [*Imagining a headline:*] "Oedipus Rex, Tragic Hero."

OEDIPUS: I like the sound of that!

CREON: We'll start working on a speech for you immediately, my lord.

OEDIPUS: It must be brilliant, Creon.

CREON: It *will* be brilliant.

JOCASTA: And what will this speech say about us, about me?

OEDIPUS: Oh...right.

[JOCASTA *looks at* OEDIPUS. *He's uncomfortable looking back.*]

JOCASTA: If you really want me to go, I don't want to be a burden. I'll just go.

[JOCASTA *begins to leave.*]

OEDIPUS: Let the speech say...I cannot, and will not, apologize for marrying the greatest woman I've ever known!

JOCASTA: You mean it?

OEDIPUS: I love you, Jocasta, and true love is as Greek as mom, the flag and spinach pie.

JOCASTA: Oh, Oedi, darling!

OEDIPUS: Jocasta, my love!

JOCASTA: My hero!

OEDIPUS: My dearest!

JOCASTA: Sweetie! [OEDIPUS *and* JOCASTA *embrace warmly.*]

[*We hear:*]

TOWN CRIER: [*O.S.*] Hear ye, hear ye! Love conquers all! And when I say all, believe me, I mean all!

[*The lights fade.*]

THE END

Jacquelyn Reingold

CREATIVE DEVELOPMENT

Jacquelyn Reingold

Jacquelyn Reingold's newest play, *Acapulco*, was part of the Bay Street Theatre's 1998 reading series. Her play, *Girl Gone*, was produced off-Broadway by the MCC Theatre, and then in 1996 at the City Garage in Los Angeles. It received the Kennedy Center's Fund for New American Plays Roger Stevens Award, and is published in *Women Playwrights: The Best Plays of 1994*. Her one-acts, *Dear Kenneth Blake* and *Tunnel of Love*, were produced in Ensemble Studio Theatre Marathons, received Drama-Logue Awards for their Los Angeles productions, and are published in *The Best American Short Plays 1996-97* and *1994-95*.

Jacquelyn's other plays which include *Freeze Tag, Lost and Found, A.M.L.*, and *Joe and Stew* have been seen in New York at Ensemble Studio Theatre, Naked Angels, MCC Theatre, Primary Stages, the Working Theatre, the Circle Rep Lab, and at theatres across the country, and in London. Her work has been published by Dramatists Play Service, Samuel French, Smith and Kraus, and in *The Quarterly*. She has written and directed plays for inner city kids at the 52nd Street Project, and is a member playwright of New Dramatists and Ensemble Studio Theatre. Her screenplay adaptation of *Girl Gone* has been optioned by Beech Hill Films, to be directed by Kevin Bacon.

Creative Development was first produced by the Shadowbox Theatre in Columbus, Ohio.

Characters:

DOUG BELLOWS, 65. The creative director for an important film company. Animated, intense, volatile.

DIANE/ISIS, 30. Posing as a playwright, really a goddess. Bright, sharp, strong.

TIME: *Now.*

PLACE: *Here.*

SETTING: *A nice office. Plastic palm tree.* DOUG BELLOWS *sits at his desk. He picks up a piece of paper, looks at it for a second, puts it down. A woman enters. She wears a coat.*

DOUG: Hello, hello. Come in, come in.

DIANE: Hi.

DOUG: Have a seat. Nice to meet you.

DIANE: Thank you for calling.

DOUG: Always like to meet young writers. Take off your coat.

DIANE: That's ok.

DOUG: You cold? [*She nods.*] Damn, I'm sweating up a storm up here. Water? [*He opens a bottle of Evian, she pulls a glass out of her bag.*]

DIANE: Thank you.

DOUG: Well. Hmm. [*He pours some water into her glass. They drink.*] So uh uh [*He looks at his paper.*] Dierdre.

DIANE: Donna.

DOUG: Yes. I'm Doug.

DIANE: Right.

DOUG: Bellows.

DIANE: Yes.

DOUG: Let's be frank, Donna, your play is not a movie.

DIANE: Oh?

DOUG: No, your play, I'm afraid, is definitely a play. And a play is almost never going to be a movie.

DIANE: Well, I thought....

DOUG: Now I didn't actually see your play.

DIANE: Oh?

DOUG: Oh, I tried, but it was raining, dear.

DIANE: Uh huh.

DOUG: Do you know what it's like to get a cab in the rain? It's hell.

DIANE: Maybe you could come another night.

DOUG: I thought it was over. [*He looks at his paper.*]

DIANE: It's been extended.

DOUG: Oh, well. How did that happen?

DIANE: Word of mouth, people liking it, that sort of thing.

DOUG: I see. Well, I'm sure it'll close soon, don't you think?

DIANE: No, actually I'm hoping it'll run for a very long time.

DOUG: Ha ha ha, I doubt that.

DIANE: I'd be happy to get you tickets.

DOUG: It's my wife, she can't make it.

DIANE: Maybe you could come without her. [*She pulls a ticket out of her bag.*]

DOUG: Now, Donna, the point is, regardless, it's not a movie. I've read the coverage. [*He holds the paper over his head, he chuckles.*] And it's not a movie. I mean what does it have? Live people talking to each other? Ha. Now, is there anyone famous in it?

DIANE: No.

DOUG: I know this may be hard to hear, and you seem like a particularly lovely young person. See, I used to be in the theatre, I was an actor once, a very good one, very, you know, good, and well I gave it up and I'm much better off now. It's really a pleasure to meet you. Sure you won't take off that coat? [*She shakes her head no.*] Can I get you anything? Cappucino?

DIANE: Thank you, I have my own. [*She pulls a cappucino out of her bag.*]

DOUG: Hmm. So. Uh, [*He presses his buzzer.*] Cappucino, one. Donna, now. Hmm, I'm sure your play was nice, very uh interesting, but I bet it didn't pay the rent, did it, and how many people actually saw it, right? I know you wouldn't be here if you weren't interested in writing movies. Everyone wants to go to the movies, and everyone wants to do movies. It's well, something magical.

[*A hand appears in the doorway holding a cappucino. He retrieves it.* DIANE *offers him a shaker of cinnamon from her bag.*]

DOUG: Uh. Thanks.

DIANE: Mr. Bellows.

DOUG: Doug, please.

DIANE: Doug, you have some foam. On your mouth.

DOUG: Oh. Thank you. So you gotta understand the hell we're in here. The people I work for are big powerful people, and they want big powerful movies. High concept. Now your play, if we made it into a movie, which we never would, would be an art film, and no one wants an art film and if they say they do they're a big fat liar. Ha! Let me introduce you to someone. [*He presses a buzzer.*] Send in Stew. I'm gonna do you a big favor.

[*A door opens.* STEW'S *shadow is seen.*]

DOUG: Stew, this is a writer, a playwright. [STEW *leaves.*] Never turn down a meeting, that's how things happen. So, where was I?

DIANE: My play.

DOUG: Right. By the way, how did you get it produced?

DIANE: Excuse me?

DOUG: How did you get that theatre to do your play? What exactly did you have to do?

DIANE: I think they liked it.

DOUG: Really? Huh. See I used to be in the theatre, I was a director, did some very interesting, you know, unusual non literary, I mean non linear work, maybe you know of it. Anyway, now I'm lucky enough to be here and help out playwrights like yourself. 'Cause I can tell by the cut of your coat I make a pretty penny more than you, dear. Would you like to read some screenplays? We have quite a collection.

DIANE: Have you produced any of these?

DOUG: What?

DIANE: What movies have you actually produced here?

DOUG: Donna! Are you with me?

DIANE: Yes.

DOUG: I'm going to tell you something very important now. About how to sell a movie. Are you listening?

DIANE: I'm listening.

DOUG: [*Clearly.*] The only way to make a movie is to make one that's already been made. You got it?

DIANE: Maybe you could say it again. A little louder.

DOUG: The only way to make a movie is to make one that's already been made! Like like Gump. [*He jumps up.*] *Gump.* Do you have a *Gump*? I gotta get a Gump.

DIANE: Um.

DOUG: Gump. I need a Gump. Do you have a Gump Gump Gump.

DIANE: Are you all right?

DOUG: Yes Gump I'm all right Gump of course I'm all right why wouldn't I be all right?

DIANE: I'm going to go out on a limb here and tell you it's very important that you see my play.

DOUG: What? What are you talking about?

DIANE: We could go right now.

DOUG: What?

DIANE: I strongly suggest it.

DOUG: No.

DIANE: How about another play?

DOUG: Excuse me?

DIANE: Why not?

DOUG: Look, I think I've made my point here. Are you interested in pitching or what? Do you have any big ideas?

DIANE: My play.

DOUG: You're not getting the message. Why are you not getting the message?

DIANE: Come to my play.

DOUG: No way.

DIANE: I'm warning you.

DOUG: You're warning me — very funny — the nerve. This is my office.

DIANE: What are you afraid of, huh?

DOUG: Afraid? What do I have to be afraid of?

DIANE: Then why not?

DOUG: Because because I don't go to the theatre. All right? Why should I? No one goes. Who goes? Tourists? Other people in the theatre? It's pathetic, it's elitist, it's too expensive, you can't eat popcorn, you can't go to the bathroom until intermission and nowadays a play doesn't even have an intermisson. Does yours?

DIANE: No.

DOUG: See? I have a very small bladder. [*She hands him a urinal from her bag. He grabs it and uses it for emphasis.*] Hell no I won't go. It's dying, it's dead. You know that. Everyone does. So give it up. Wake up. Donna!!! Wake up!! There is no theatre anymore, it's a dinosaur on its last fart. Who goes...no one! Stop with the plays, start with the blockbusters. Gump Gump Gump! [*Very calm:*] So, I'm sure if you have something like like that movie I mentioned I'm sure we could work together, collaborate. Very nicely. Very successfully.

DIANE: Bellows.

DOUG: Yes?

DIANE: I'm not really a playwright.

DOUG: Thank God, I didn't think you were. You certainly don't act like one.

DIANE: My name isn't Donna.

DOUG: Oh?

DIANE: It's Diane.

[*Thunder and lightning as she pulls off her coat, revealing a mini toga. She is a powerful goddess.*]

DIANE: Diane Isis. You just failed the last test.

DOUG: Very funny ha ha.

DIANE: I'm not kidding, Doug.

DOUG: Who put you up to this, Stew? That guy. [*He presses a buzzer.*]

DIANE: There is no more Stew.

DOUG: Yeah, right, good one.

DIANE: Do you hear that? [*She opens her bag, we hear lovely singing.*] Those are the muses, all nine of them, they've been listening to your every word, and they can't believe what they've heard.

DOUG: Oh, I'm shaking. What did I do?

DIANE: Impersonated a creative director.

DOUG: I am a creative director.

DIANE: Ha!

DOUG: Is this some kind of a pitch? A feminist Spartacus remake? Well, it's not working.

DIANE: Bellows! Did you think you could get away with it? Did you think no one was watching? Calling in thousands of playwrights to humiliate them, to convince them to stop writing plays and start writing movies?

DOUG: Now look Dierdre Donna Diane I have another meeting in a minute so.

DIANE: You're telling writers what to do? Isn't that a little upside down, Doug? Shouldn't it really be the other way around, Doug?

[*A ferocious wind blows.* DOUG *holds onto his desk for dear life.*]

DOUG: What the hell was that?

DIANE: That was Calliope exhaling.

DOUG: Ok ok, this meeting is over.

DIANE: This meeting has just begun!!!!

DOUG: What are you after? A deal? Well fine, let's hear it.

DIANE: Your deal days are done, Doug. You've turned the artistic world upside down and we're here to set it straight and the first casualty is you.

DOUG: Have we met before?

DIANE: You hear that? [*We hear hissing.*] Those are the sisters they're morphing into something a little more s-s-sinister.

DOUG: Hey, I'm just doing my job.

DIANE: We know all about your job, what you really do here. The underground network, the antitheatre lobbying effort, the I Won't Go To The Theatre Newsletter. And we are not amused. We know you've converted millions, and raised money into the billions. We know who you contributed to in the last election. We know all about you.

DOUG: I got nothing to hide. Maybe that was me, but I'm not killing the theatre, I'm just helping it go easy. I'm protecting audiences all over the world from an intolerable night out. What are you gonna do? Fire me? Go ahead, There'll be someone else here tomorrow.

DIANE: Why'd you do it, Doug? Fear? Was that it? Afraid of seeing something that might make you uncomfortable? Well, you're about to learn the real meaning of the word. Sisters!

[*From out of her bag emerge nine women of all shapes and sizes. They all wear mini togas with a large M on them, and have snakes in their hair.*]

DOUG: Well, uh hello, uh, ladies.

DIANE: Prepare for your final treatment. We have come for our revenge.

MUSES & DIANE: [*They roar at him.*] Rah!

[*The lights change.*]

DOUG: Now hang on, let's be reasonable here.

[*They surround him, and they tie him up.*]

MUSES: [*They roar.*] Rah!

DOUG: Now now look what are you doing? I mean, I get it, ok? You made your point. Hey! Please. I'm just human, right? I mean do you know how hard it is to make a living in the theatre?

[*They pull out their weapons. One has a giant paintbrush, one has a musical instrument, one has a big pair of toe shoes, another a chisel. DIANE pulls out a mirror. They start to create something.*]

DOUG: Ok, what do you want? I'll let you make an art film, ok? You can make that Dierdre's play into a very arty art film. We can work together, do things from the inside. I know where you're coming from. I used to be in the theatre. I was a producer. Not for profit!

[*The MUSES and DIANE have created an instant stage for DOUG.*]

DIANE: Ok, Bellows. Create.

DOUG: What?

DIANE: You're in a theatre, you're on the stage.

DOUG: What?

DIANE: You've got an audience.

[*House lights come up.*]

DOUG: Oh my God, I do.

DIANE: It's live. Create. Write a poem, recite a play, do a dance. They're waiting.

DOUG: [*To audience.*] Uh. Hello. Uh. [*To* DIANE] Ok, I'll call those playwrights. I'll call every playwright and apologize. Diane? Oh God, Diane? [*To audience*] Ha ha ha. Uh. Uh. [*To* DIANE) I'll cancel the committee. I was wrong. I admit it. I was a jerk. Diane? [*To audience*] Uh uh. [*The muses as audience start to cough, unwrap candy wrappers, shuffle, and answer their ringing cell phones.*) [*To* DIANE] Think of my wife. My kids. I have daughters, one does modern dance, the other plays the piano, I swear. Uh.. Uh.. I can't. Please. I can't. I'm not creative. I'm not. I have no ideas. None. None.

DIANE: This is your life now, Doug. For eternity this is what you will be: an actor/director/producer on stage without a play. Forever.

DOUG: Oh God. Look, ok, this is very hard for me, but I'll go to the play. I will, I'll go to that Donna's play. Please! Forgive me. My life is hell. You have to understand. I'm the one who turned down Gump. [*He sobs.*] It's true. For ten years I said no to Gump. And look what happened.

DIANE: Doug, wasn't that some years ago?

DOUG: Yes, but but I haven't been able to get past it.

MUSE 1: [*A young muse speaks*] Wow.

MUSE 2:[*A large muse speaks*] Gump.

MUSE 3: [*An old muse*] That's bad.

MUSE 4: [*A dim muse*] Really bad.

MUSE 5: [*A loud muse*] Yeah.

MUSE 6: [*A silly muse*] I can't believe he did that.

MUSE 7: [*A fast muse*] Talk about stupid.

MUSE 8: [*A sloppy muse*] Dumb.

MUSE 9: [*A muse like muse*] Pathetic.

ALL MUSES: [*All the muses*] Maybe he's suffered enough.

[*They look to* DIANE, *she thinks.*]

DOUG: I have. Really. I have. And look, uh ladies, I mean we've come a long way since you were last here. We've developed, creatively. Right? I mean, compassion and all that, forgiveness. [*They look at each other.*] I said I'd go to the play,. I mean isn't that the point? I mean. I will go. Why we can all go. I mean, have you seen that play? [*The muses look away, embarrassed.*] We can go together: you, me; man, uh women; the past, the present. Group rate. How's that?

[*The lights brighten. A reprieve.*]

DIANE: Hmm. Untie him.

[*They start to slowly untie him.* DIANE *puts on her coat.*]

DOUG: Oh thank you, thank you. You won't regret it. From now on I'll be different. I swear. Very different.

DIANE: Hmm, Doug.

DOUG: Yeah?

DIANE: One more thing.

DOUG: What is it, dear?

DIANE: I have this idea.

DOUG: Really?

DIANE: For a movie. Blockbuster. I thought I'd just try it out on you.

DOUG: Oh?

DIANE: It's about a guy who dresses as a woman. An unattractive woman.

DOUG: It's been done.

DIANE: Exactly. It takes place on a sinking boat.

DOUG: That's been done, sounds good.

DIANE: Special effects from a natural disaster.

DOUG: Yeah

DIANE: A plot from Shakespeare.

DOUG: I'm listening.

DIANE: A fatal illness.

DOUG: Uh huh.

DIANE: And the thing is…The main character, the one dressed as the very unattractive woman, he's also dumb.

DOUG: Oh.

DIANE: Very dumb.

DOUG: Yeah?

DIANE: Stupid.

DOUG: Uh huh.

DIANE: Ugly.

DOUG: I see.

DIANE: And we can call it…

DOUG: What? What?

DIANE: We can call it. Frump.

DOUG: FRUMP! I love it! We'll make it.

DIANE: Tie him up! [*They roar.*] Rah!

   [DIANE *throws off her coat, weapons come out. Blackout.*]

THE END

Murray Schisgal

THE MAN WHO COULDN'T STOP CRYING

Murray Schisgal

Murray Schisgal [*playwright*] has had six plays produced on Broadway, a good many Off-Broadway, Off-Off-Broadway, and in regional theatre. He was nominated for a Tony for his play *Luv*, an Oscar for co-writing the film *Tootsie*, and his original television screenplay, *The Love Song of Barney Kempinski* won an Emmy. His other credits include *The Typists and the Tiger*, which received the Outer Circle and Vernon Rice awards. He is a producer for Punch Productions. He has co-produced two feature films for them: *A Walk On the Moon*, [Miramax], and *The Devil's Arithmetic*, [Showtime].

SETTING: *The Central Park West apartment of* PAMELA *and* MAR-
      CELLO SEGAL.

TIME: *Sunday morning.*

AT RISE: *The living room. Entrance door in right wall; doors to the
      kitchen and bedroom in left wall; a panoramic, linen-shaded
      window overlooking the park in rear wall.*

    *The area near the kitchen has been furnished to serve as a
    dinette. On a buffet table, platters of breakfast food, condiments,
    utensils, a coffeemaker and a Tiffany vase filled with vibrantly
    bright flowers.* MARCELLO *is seated in an armchair, reading the
    morning Times. He is wearing a Gucci bathrobe over his scrupu-
    lously tailored slacks and shirt. He is sniffling, rubbing his wet
    eyes with the heel of his hand.*

PAMELA: [*O.S.*] Marcello?

MARCELLO: Yes, dear?

PAMELA: [*O.S.*] Are you crying?

MARCELLO: [*Tries fiercely to stop sniffling.*] No, dear. I have a frog in
    my throat!

PAMELA: [*O.S.*] Would you like a lozenge?

MARCELLO: Not before breakfast, sweetheart.

    [*He waits a beat to hear if she's going to say more. She doesn't. He
    inhales deeply; sighs with relief. He looks about the room. Every-
    thing seems normal. He returns to the newspaper, matter-of-factly.
    Almost at once, he starts whimpering, ever so softly. As he contin-
    ues reading, his whimpering becomes more intense, if not louder.*]

PAMELA: [*O.S.*] Marcello!

MARCELLO: [*Whimpering in spite of his efforts not to.*] I'm not crying,
    darling!

PAMELA: [*O.S.*] Then what is that noise in there?

MARCELLO: The radiators! The super is sending up steam!

PAMELA: [*O.S.*] In the middle of June?

MARCELLO: I suspect he's reminding us Christmas is coming soon!

[*He waits a beat to hear if she's going to say more. She doesn't. He inhales deeply; sighs with relief. He looks about the room. Everything seems normal. He returns to the newspaper, matter-of-factly. There's no holding back the tears now. He starts sobbing. Visibly annoyed,* PAMELA *enters from kitchen, carrying a lidded dish of scrambled eggs and another of toast. She places the dishes on the buffet. She is dressed in an elegant, floor-length silk robe.*]

PAMELA: Will you tell me why you're crying? Will you, please, tell me why you're crying?

MARCELLO: This...This obituary...in the newspaper. Richard... Richard Kislawski...died yesterday. They...They have no idea why he died! [*And now a torrent of sobs flows from him.*]

PAMELA: Do we know a Richard Kislawski?

MARCELLO: No. No. We never had the pleasure.

PAMELA: Then why are you crying?

MARCELLO: He was...four years younger than I am!

PAMELA: So?

MARCELLO: So he's gone! It's all over for him!

PAMELA: So?

MARCELLO: So, for the same money it could have been me! You could have lost me four years ago!

PAMELA: But I didn't lose you! You're sitting here, in the living room, waiting for your scrambled eggs and toast!

MARCELLO: By happenstance! By sheer happenstance! If I went like Richard Kislawski, I wouldn't have shared with you all the...all the wonderful, wonderful times we had together these last four years!

PAMELA: What wonderful times are you referring to?

MARCELLO: What's that?

PAMELA: What were the wonderful times?

MARCELLO: Pamela, it was only two years ago we took our fantastic trip to China, don't you remember?

PAMELA: Of course, I remember. I spent a whole week in a Beijing hospital with a bronchial infection!

MARCELLO: That was just one week of eight wonderful, wonderful days and…and what about the incredibly beautiful time we spent in Nova Scotia?

PAMELA: Nova Scotia?

MARCELLO: Where we ate smoked salmon!

PAMELA: Oh, yes, of course, but, Marcello, it rained practically everyday…

MARCELLO: Are you putting me down?

PAMELA: [*Fervently.*] No!

MARCELLO: It sounds like it. You're saying that the trips I planned over the last four years have been total disasters!

PAMELA: That's not what I'm saying, darling. I'm saying you planned unbelievably wonderful trips! But they weren't to China and Nova Scotia. They were to Paris last New Year's and St. Petersburg the previous winter, and the two glorious weeks we spent cruising the Greek Islands. You're being too sensitive.

MARCELLO: [*Perhaps.*] If I had passed away four years ago, I wouldn't have been at Denny's wedding.

PAMELA: And I would have been inconsolably bereaved.

MARCELLO: I wouldn't have known Denny's wife.

PAMELA: She's a very special young woman.

MARCELLO: I wouldn't even have known she was six months pregnant when she married Denny! [*He breaks into a fresh torrent of sobs.* PAMELA *pulls the hassock to his armchair; sits on it.*]

PAMELA: Shhh. Shhh. That's enough. No more crying, *please.*

[*She wipes his tearing eyes with handkerchief.*]

Sweetheart, you have to stop. I can't go on living like this. It's become an absolute nightmare for me.

MARCELLO: Rich...Richard Kislawski. He had no wife...no family ...and...and...the most depressing part...they're...they're burying him in New Jersey!

[*A burst of sobs.*]

PAMELA: Shhh. Shhh. You're too sensitive. You're too sympathetic. You're too caring. I know how difficult it is for you to control your emotions. But it's getting worse, infinitely worse. We have to put an end to your crying or...I don't know how we can go on living together.

MARCELLO: You...You'd leave me?

PAMELA: If I answer you honestly, do you promise not to cry?

MARCELLO: I promise.

PAMELA: I would leave you. I'd have to. To save my sanity and my self-respect.

[*And* MARCELLO *starts bawling his head off. He rises from arm-chair, paces, wags his body back and forth in a paroxysm of grief.*]

PAMELA: [*Cont'd.*] Marcello, you promised...!

MARCELLO: It's so sad! We've been married for twenty-seven years! We've been so happy! I love you! You're the only woman I ever loved, and now...now...[*In high, shrill voice.*]...it's all going down the toilet!

PAMELA: Why are you hysterical? I merely said I would leave you if you didn't stop crying. But if you did stop crying, we would continue living together. Isn't that what you want?

MARCELLO: More than anything. I love you. I don't want to lose you.

PAMELA: Then let's deal with this intelligently and rationally. First of all, do you agree that you're financially well-off and incredibly successful?

MARCELLO: [*Emphatically.*] I do!

PAMELA: And may I ask how you became financially well-off and incredibly successful?

MARCELLO: Your father gave me two-hundred and fifty thousand dollars!

PAMELA: That's not what I'm driving at.

MARCELLO: Forgive me!

PAMELA: Besides, my father didn't give you two-hundred and fifty thousand dollars; he loaned it to you, and you repaid it with interest. What I *was* driving at was that you opened, in a single decade, nineteen express photo shops that have proven to be an absolute phenomenon in discount marketing. And you did all of it by yourself, do you agree?

MARCELLO: I do!

PAMELA: Then answer me this: if you're a relatively young, healthy, successful millionaire who has a loving, devoted family, why are you continually crying?

MARCELLO: Are you putting me down?

PAMELA: No, sweetheart, I'm not. I'm merely asking you a question.

MARCELLO: [*Perhaps.*] I am not continually crying, to answer your question. As a matter of fact, other than this morning, I can't remember the last time I cried.

PAMELA: You can't.

MARCELLO: I can't.

PAMELA: Then answer me this: where were we last night?

MARCELLO: Last night we went to the movies.

PAMELA: And what movie did we see?

MARCELLO: A comedy. With what's-his-name.

PAMELA: Did you enjoy it?

[MARCELLO *moves to buffet table. He transfers scrambled eggs and toast onto a dish and sits down at the dinette table to eat his breakfast. Soon after,* PAMELA *joins him at table to have her breakfast.*]

MARCELLO: Enormously. It was hilarious. What was it called?

PAMELA: *"The Nutty Professor."* With Eddie Murphy.

MARCELLO: He was brilliant. How they changed his character from an obese monstrosity to a thin, handsome man was technologically amazing.

PAMELA: You cried.

MARCELLO: I what?

PAMELA: You cried during the entire movie.

MARCELLO: Pamela, please, be fair. I couldn't stop laughing! It was so funny...I'm laughing right now just thinking about it.

[*He breaks into a not quite believable laugh.*]

PAMELA: Marcello, look at me. Look at me a moment.

MARCELLO: [*Suspiciously.*] Why?

PAMELA: Because I asked you.

MARCELLO: You sound hostile.

PAMELA: I swear to you, I am not hostile.

MARCELLO: You don't realize how strongly you come on at times.

PAMELA: If I sounded hostile or came on too strongly, I sincerely apologize.

MARCELLO: [*Perhaps she's sincere.*] I'm looking at you. As you requested.

PAMELA: You cried during the entire movie last night.

MARCELLO: You heard me?

PAMELA: No, I didn't. You've become something of an expert at repressing the noises that usually accompany crying. In the movies you cry soundlessly.

MARCELLO: Then how do you know...[*"I was crying?"*]

PAMELA: I've become something of an expert, too. Last night when the movie was over and the lights went on, I turned to you before you could turn away from me. Your eyes were drowning in a Niagara of tears.

MARCELLO: [*Head bowed in defeat.*] I couldn't help myself. I empathized with the Eddie Murphy character. I frequently feel that I have two personalities of my own. One is aggressive and egocentric. The other is timid, insecure, and frightened of everthing.

PAMELA: Darling, dearest, I don't want you to feel miserable. I don't. But you have to acknowledge the truth, and the truth is that whenever we go to a movie, regardless of what it's about, you cry. You cry, my sweet, dear husband, every single time we go to a movie.

MARCELLO: [*A thoughtful beat.*] Let me modify what I said previously. Other than this morning and...

PAMELA: You also cry every single time we go to a wedding.

MARCELLO: Noooo.

PAMELA: Yes, you do. You can't hide your tears from me. I'm wise to your ways.

MARCELLO: When was the last wedding we went to?

PAMELA: David and Melissa's.

MARCELLO: And I...[*"Cried?"*]

PAMELA: Yes, you did. During the ceremony. It was shamefully embarrassing. Everyone turned to stare at you.

MARCELLO: Pam, they were so young. They were practically babies. And when David said to Melissa, "This day I will marry my friend...

[*He starts sobbing;* PAMELA *hands him a handkerchief.*]

...the one I laugh with, the one I live for, the one I dream for and...will...love...forever..."

[*A few more sobs before gaining control.*]

I...I'm only human. Lots of people cry at weddings.

PAMELA: Yes, they do. I cry, sometimes, but you cry all the time. And, incidentally, you also cry at parades.

MARCELLO: [*Incredulously.*] Parades? I cry at parades?

PAMELA: Yes, you do. All the time.

MARCELLO: Are you talking about the Memorial Day parade for the men and women who sacrificed their lives for our country?

PAMELA: No, I'm talking about every parade, including the Irish parade, the Israeli parade, the gay and lesbian parade, and the Macy's Thanksgiving Day parade!

MARCELLO: [*A thoughtful beat.*] Let me modify what I said previously. Other than this morning and last night and whenever we go to a movie or to a wedding or to a parade, I can't remember the last time I cried.

PAMELA: Do you see that band-aid on your finger?

MARCELLO: This?

PAMELA: Yes. Why is it on your finger?

MARCELLO: I cut myself.

PAMELA: When?

MARCELLO: Was it yesterday?

PAMELA: No, it was the day before yesterday, Friday. You were cutting a bagel for breakfast, the knife slipped and you cut your finger.

MARCELLO: You're right. It was the day before yesterday, Friday.

PAMELA: You cried?

MARCELLO: Are you serious?

PAMELA: You did cry.

MARCELLO: So what's so extraordinary about that? I assume if I cut my finger I was in pain, so I cried. Perfectly normal. I'll modify what I said previously. Other than this morning and last night and whenever we go to a movie or to a wedding or to a parade, and the day before yesterday, Friday, when I cut my finger, I can't remember the last time I cried!

PAMELA: Do you remember what we did Thursday night?

MARCELLO: Do we have to go on with this senseless...?

PAMELA: We had dinner at home, and after dinner we looked through an old scrapbook you found in the closet. Do you remember that?

MARCELLO: I'm not retarded. In spite of your accusations. There were photographs in it of summers we spent in East Hampton. When Denny was growing up.

PAMELA: He was a baby the first summer we went out there. The last summer we spent there was just before he went off to college.

MARCELLO: They were...Oh, God, they were wonderful summers.

PAMELA: You and Denny were inseparable.

MARCELLO: Remember when we'd get up at five in the morning to go off fishing on Captain Bob's boat?

PAMELA: You didn't get back until after sunset!

MARCELLO: With a bag full of bass and blues and flounders ...

PAMELA: Don't forget the times the three of us went bowling or to the carnivals in Southhampton!

MARCELLO: How about when we'd drive out to Montauk and have those delicious steamers and creamy lobster rolls at Gosman's?

PAMELA: Did you notice the photograph of Denny pitching in the Artists and Writers game?

MARCELLO: He was only fourteen years old.

PAMELA: When he struck out Kurt Vonnegut and then Joseph Heller, the crowd screamed like nothing I ever heard before.

MARCELLO: I swear to you, Pam, if that boy had wanted, he could have been a professional ballplayer.

PAMELA: You cried.

MARCELLO: What's that?

PAMELA: You cried last Thursday. When we were looking through the old scrapbook.

[MARCELLO *throws his napkin on the table; rises; paces indignantly.*]

MARCELLO: I cried, yes! I confess it! I acknowledge it!

PAMELA: Marcello, why are you raising your voice? We said we'd deal with this intelligently and...

MARCELLO: Deal with it any way you want! I've had enough of your criticisms!

PAMELA: Criticisms?

MARCELLO: Yes, criticisms, criticisms, criticisms! That's all I've been hearing! But you are not going to prevent me from expressing my feelings! You accuse me of crying when we looked at those photographs last Thursday. How could I not cry? We had a family! There were three of us! Inseparable! Sharing for eighteen years adventures and trips and parties and joyous, festive holidays! So what happened? Where did everything go to? Where did our family go to? Our boy leaves us for college at eighteen, he comes back four years later to move into his own apartment, he starts a career in the impenetrable canyons of Wall Street, marries a girl we barely know, has a child we barely know, and that's it, that's the whole ball of wax! No more sharing! No more celebrating! Thanks for the memory, folks!

PAMELA: Darling, be reasonable. Our family is no different from countless other families. Children grow up and start families of their own. What was, was. And Denny does visit; he does call; he...

MARCELLO: [*Sits on sofa.*] Empty gestures. The heartache that boy has caused me...

PAMELA: Stop it now. I am not going to let you blame Denny for your...for your own...sickness! Yes, that's what it is, a sickness! And if you persist in not seeing a doctor, you force me to...

MARCELLO: I saw a doctor!

PAMELA: What doctor?

MARCELLO: My doctor! Doctor Gutenberg!

PAMELA: But Doctor Gutenberg is an ophthalmologist!

MARCELLO: And he explained everything to me quite intelligently and quite rationally!

PAMELA: He explained why you...[*"Cry?"*]

MARCELLO: Yes!

PAMELA: [*Sits in armchair.*] This I'd like to hear. What did he say?

MARCELLO: He said I have a blockage of my tear ducts and that's what causes my eyes to tear all the time. It's purely physiological.

PAMELA: Blockage of your tear ducts causes you to cry?

MARCELLO: Yes!

PAMELA: Nonsense! Poppycock! First of all, you do not cry all the time. You cry at specific times as a consequence of specific events. For example, you cried today because you read the obituary of Richard Kislawski. You cried last night because you saw a movie. You cried Friday because you cut your finger. And so on and so forth. If the cause of your crying was physiological, as you say, you wouldn't require a specific event to trigger it.

MARCELLO: Does this give you pleasure?

PAMELA: What pleasure?

MARCELLO: Hounding me. Abusing me. Is it that you want me to feel utterly miserable before putting an end to your hostility?

[PAMELA *moves to sit beside him on sofa.*]

PAMELA: Darling, don't say it, please. You're hurting me. If there's anything in the world I want it's to love you and spend the remainder of my days with you. But there are things I can't deal with either. I can't go on pretending we're living a normal life together. I beg you, I plead with you, please, please, see a psychiatrist!

MARCELLO: You've made your point. But I am not so sick that I'm unaware of your relentless assault on my shortcomings.

PAMELA: You take everything I say as criticism. I am not criticizing you. I am trying to help you, can't you understand that?

MARCELLO: Understand, yes. Condone, no. It may be that I need a psychiatrist. I don't want to argue about it now. I have something to ask of you.

PAMELA: Anything. Ask me anything.

MARCELLO: Trust me. Have faith in me. Like you used to. When we were first married. I am not incapable of resolve and will-power.

PAMELA: Don't even think it! What you've done with your life, what you've accomplished...I don't know of any man who started out as you did, literally penniless and directionless, and who went on to achieve as much as you have.

MARCELLO: Then trust me on this. Let me deal with the problem in my own way. I promise you, my crying jags are over. I will no longer burden you with this...aberration of mine.

PAMELA: I believe you. I trust you. Unreservedly. Oh, hold me, sweetheart. Hold me tightly, tightly.

[*He does so.*]

PAMELA: [*Cont'd.*] It feels so good to be in your arms. I'm the luckiest woman in the world!

[*Pulls away.*]

PAMELA: Let's do something! Let's go out! Let's walk in the park, spend an hour at the Met...They have this glorious Byzantium show on! Afterwards, we can have lunch at the Stanhope!

MARCELLO: I just have to put on a jacket. You get dressed.

PAMELA: I love you.

MARCELLO: I love you.

PAMELA: [*Hugs him.*] I do, I do, I do! [*Kisses him quickly, noisily; rises.*] I won't be long.

[*She moves into the bedroom, closing door behind her.*
MARCELLO inhales deeply; sighs with relief. He looks about the room. Everything seems normal.
He picks up remote control from coffee table and clicks on dinette stereo, radio station WQXR. He returns remote to coffee table.
For a beat or two there is no sound.
MARCELLO rises from sofa, moves to buffet table for a cup of coffee.]

The music begins to play. It's Tomaso Albinoni's "Adagio in G Minor." Or some such affecting, funereal piece.

MARCELLO *stops in his stride. He listens, attentively, as the initial chords reverberate, quietly, in the room.*

A profound sense of his own mortality stuns MARCELLO. *The color drains from his face, which gradually turns into a mask of grief and foreboding. His shoulders collapse.*

Ashes to ashes. Dust to dust.

Vanity. All is vanity.

He moves back and forth across the room, his shoes scraping the carpet as if he hasn't the strength to lift them. His head bows; his arms dangle uselessly at his sides.

Woe is me. Woe is me.

So softly at first that we mistake the sound for the faint stirrings of a summer breeze, MARCELLO *starts moaning.*

The moaning drifts into wailing and the wailing into sobbing.

Suddenly remembering his promise to PAMELA, *he turns to the bedroom door, clamps his hand over his mouth.* PAMELA *mustn't hear him!*

But he can't stifle the sobs that pour out from between his fingers.

And the incessantly mournful music continues to feed his "abberation."

He falls to his knees, clamps his second hand over his first hand, which still covers his mouth.

To no avail. On his knees, he moves rapidly to the right wall. He pushes his face to the floorboard to muffle his sobs or, perhaps, he presses his face under a piece of furniture that is against the right wall.

PAMELA *mustn't hear him!*

But there's no stopping the sobbing.

It increases with the increasingly lugubrious, dirge-like adagio.

He must shut off the damn stereo! Where's the remote control?

He rolls over on his back, searches through his bathrobe and pants pockets, twisting, turning, lifting legs into air.

All the while he's sobbing.

PAMELA *enters, dressed to go out. She stares at* MARCELLO, *grimly.*

He freezes. His legs are still up in the air. On his back, MARC-
ELLO'S *eyes meet* PAMELA'S.

*His sobbing rises a few notches. Now he really has cause to cry.
He's broken his promise to* PAMELA.

*He gets to his feet, spots the remote on the coffee table and shuts
off the stereo.*

*He blows his nose into a handkerchief as he moves to sit down
on the sofa. He sobs a bit more before gaining control of himself.]*

PAMELA: Do you promise to see a psychiatrist now?

MARCELLO: It won't help.

PAMELA: Is that another evasion of yours?

MARCELLO: No. I've seen a psychiatrist.

PAMELA: You did?

MARCELLO: Yes.

PAMELA: When?

MARCELLO: When Denny got married.

PAMELA: Why didn't you tell me?

MARCELLO: Because I was embarrassed. Because I hated her.

PAMELA: The psychiatrist, I take it, is a woman.

MARCELLO: Doctor Madeline DeKoker. Doctor Gutenberg recom-
mended her.

PAMELA: But you stopped seeing her. Why did you hate her?

MARCELLO: I got worse instead of better. She'd make me talk about
my parents, my childhood, my relationship with girls in high
school and…I'd end up crying the whole forty-five minutes I
was with her!

PAMELA: How long did you go to her?

MARCELLO: A couple of months.

PAMELA: That's hardly long enough to deal with your…

MARCELLO: I saw another psychiatrist after her.

PAMELA: How could you not tell me any of this? I'm living with
you! Every day I see you! I…!

MARCELLO: Is that he only way you can express yourself? With abuse and hostility? Can't you show a little compassion for what I've been going through?

PAMELA: Sweetheart...

MARCELLO: Don't patronize me.

PAMELA: I wouldn't. I...

MARCELLO: You sound masculine when you use that tone of voice.

PAMELA: I didn't realize it. I'm sorry. But, sweetheart, I have every right to be annoyed. I had no idea about any of these psychiatrists. Will you, please, tell me who you saw after Doctor DeKoker?

MARCELLO: Doctor Albert Santos.

PAMELA: How long did you go to Doctor Santos?

MARCELLO: Close to a year, but it was as painful and unrewarding as my analysis with Doctor DeKoker.

PAMELA: I heard that Doctor Joshua Quenby is an excellent therapist. I can arrange...

MARCELLO: No. Twice is enough. I won't go through it again. If you'll be a little more patient with me, I promise you...

PAMELA: You said that five minutes ago. I walked out of the room to get dressed, I come back, and there you are, lying on the floor, crying your heart out.

MARCELLO: I put on the radio and there was this music...so sad, so...funereal, so...Pam, please, give me another chance, trust me!

PAMELA: I'm going down.

MARCELLO: Without me?

PAMELA: I have to think. I have to be alone for a while.

MARCELLO: [Rises.] You're coming back, aren't you?

PAMELA: I'm not going to go on living like this.

MARCELLO: Is it because I'm too sensitive, too sympathetic...too caring? Those were the words you used to describe me.

PAMELA: You go far beyond that. I'd rather leave you while I still respect you and while I still have wonderful memories of our good years together.

[*She takes a step.*]

MARCELLO: I'll see Doctor Quenby. I'll set up an appointment. I'll...

PAMELA: I'm afraid it's too late.

[*She moves to door in right wall.*]

MARCELLO: Don't go, please. We have to talk.

PAMELA: [*Without turning to him; eyes on door.*] It's useless.

MARCELLO: It's not easy living a life, sweetheart.

PAMELA: You don't make it any easier.

MARCELLO: We are getting on in years.

PAMELA: What are you driving at?

MARCELLO: The day he died, Richard Kislawski had no idea that he was going. For the same money, it could have been...

[PAMELA *abruptly turns and exits, closing door behind her.*
MARCELLO *hurries to open door, speaks to* PAMELA: *as she moves, off-stage, towards elevator.*]

MARCELLO: [*Overwrought.*] Wait! Wait! Don't ring for the elevator, sweetheart. Please. Two minutes, that's all I ask. Darling, I am going to change. There's no question about it. One can change. One has choices, free will. Throughout history we have examples...[*Horrified.*]

No, don't! Don't ring for the elevator. I am changing, sweetheart. The process has already begun. Aren't you aware of it? Haven't you noticed? I'm not crying! Do you see me crying? I have no desire to cry. There's nothing to cry about. I *am* relatively young and healthy and well-off. And I'm happy! Yes, yes, I can say it without embarrassment, I am genuinely happy! Would you like to hear me laugh, darling? I can...[*Horrified.*] Why did you press the elevator button? Don't go, not yet. Sweetheart, look at me. Listen to me. I'm laughing. I am laughing. This is not fake. [*He feigns several varieties of hearty laughter.*]

Did you hear me laughing? Did you? It's not fake. It felt wonderful! I thought I'd never be able to laugh again! But I did laugh. I did. And I am happy, honey, and I love life and I love you, darling. More than anything in the world. And, please, please, let me apologize for saying before that you sounded masculine. How stupid of me! You are definitely not masculine. You are feminine, totally and completely! You are so feminine, it frightens me, it...Where...? Where are you going? [*Horrified.*]

No, don't walk into the elevator! Don't leave without me! Wait, I'll get my jacket! Pam!

[*Off-stage, the elevator carries* PAMELA *down to the lobby. Quickly,* MARCELLO *takes off bathrobe, tosses it aside, gets jacket from the closet, puts it on, hurries to rear window, where he pulls up linen shade and opens window. During the above,* MARCELLO *performs a finger-snapping, shuffling step as he sing-songs what follows.*]

MARCELLO: I am happy. And I am glad, I am laughing 'cause I'm not sad.
Life is good,
Life is great,
Now is the time
To celebrate.

[*He stops his sing-song step and feigns several laughs before leaning out of open window; shouts:*]

MARCELLO: Pam! Here, up here! I'll meet you at the Stanhope! I'll be there in a few minutes! Okay? Love you!

[*He closes window, and resumes his finger-snapping, shuffling step as he sing-songs what follows.*]

MARCELLO: I can't be sad,
I must be glad,
To have a life,
And a loving wife.
I can't be sad,

I must be glad,
To have a life,
And a loving wife.

[*He stops his sing-song step and feigns riotous laughter as he exits,
slamming door shut behind him.*]

Shel Silverstein

THE TRIO

Shel Silverstein

Shel Silverstein was last represented on the New York stage with his play *The Devil and Billy Markham*, which played a double bill with David Mamet's *Bobby Gould in Hell*, collectively titled *Oh! Hell*, at the Mitzi Newhouse Theatre at Lincoln Center. With Mr. Mamet, he co-wrote the screenplay *Things Change* for Columbia Pictures which starred Don Ameche and Joe Mantegna. His play, *Hamlet*, was most recently performed at the Ensemble Studio Theatre in New York.

Mr. Silverstein has written and illustrated several children's classics, including *Where The Sidewalk Ends*, *A Light in the Attic*, and *The Giving Tree*. His plays include *The Crate*, *Lady or the Tiger*, *Gorilla* and *Little Feet*. He is also a noted cartoonist and the author of many songs and poems. Most recently, his song *I'm Checking Out of the Heartbreak Hotel* from the film, *Postcards From the Edge*, was nominated for an Academy Award.

An intimate restaurant. DAVID *sits at restaurant table. He studies musical score, making notes.* HELENA *sits across from him. Behind them a trio plays — three women in white dresses.*

HELENA: Well — tell me.

DAVID: Tell you what?

HELENA: What did you think of my — ?

DAVID: It was lovely

HELENA: You hated it.

DAVID: It was magnificent — you are always —

HELENA: Lovely — magnificent — everything but *right* — that's your word — *right* — I do not hear "right" — So what was not right about it?

DAVID: [*Laughs.*] You missed an arpeggio in the second movement.

HELENA: Seriously — what was not right?

DAVID: My dear, you must not interpret every —

HELENA: Don't you my dear me — Not about this. I'll be your dear later…Your darling, your — boo boo? — unless…you have other plans — [*Beat.*] You do…you have other plans…Well, then, some other night, when you —

DAVID: Jacobson is in from London. I promised him a decision about February —

HELENA: Well then. I'll see you in March.

DAVID: I meant I have to let him know about a Febru —

HELENA: I know what you meant — I was being bitchy — maybe it's the bitchiness you heard creeping into the second movement. Bitchiness *can* sound a lot like a missed arpeggio to the untrained ear. But you have such a *trained* ear — what would you do if you lost your hearing? Or if you had some horrible stroke and your right side was — *both* sides — you'd conduct with your teeth — you put that baton between your caps and shake the hell out of — that flautist — she's quite wonderful.

DAVID: Yes. They're all quite accomplished.

HELENA: There was a group playing when you first brought me here — they were playing Schopenhauer — we drank champagne — we drank to — music. "To music"…I think I know her — or I've seen her — is she well known?

DAVID: In their own circles. I imagine.

HELENA: They're quite extraordinary — for a restaurant.

DAVID: They play…competently.

HELENA: That cellist — she looks familiar.

DAVID: It's the melody. La-da — [*He hums.*]

HELENA: She looks like somebody I — doesn't she look like someone you know? [DAVID *looks.*] She's better than I am — really — she's much better than I am.

DAVID: Nonsense.

HELENA: She is — David, listen to her —

DAVID: She is not better than you are. No one is better than you are. Different — not better.

HELENA: Sometimes I think no one is better than I am — then I think *everyone* is better than I am.

DAVID: Have some of this pasta — it's extraordinary…

HELENA: I know…She looks just like that girl you used to see — what was her name? — the one with the long hair? — Marie? — Something? She had a mole on her cheek — [*He glances over.*] *She* has a mole on her cheek — [*Pause.*] What did she play? — Marie or Mona? — the one I replaced — what did she play? French horn or something.

DAVID: [*To violinist.*] Your D is flat.

VIOLINIST: [*Tunes.*] Thank you.

DAVID: Let me hum something for you — [*He does.*] Well —?

HELENA: What is this, a quiz? An aptitude test?

DAVID: None of us are above having our aptitudes tested.

HELENA: And if I guess the tune, I get what's behind curtain number three — all right — Brahma Etude Eleven — twenty-seventh measure — and I'll take the dishwasher and the trip to Hawaii — Brahms? [*She nods.*]

DAVID: What measure?

HELENA: Twenty-seventh.

DAVID: And?

HELENA: *And* the D-flat — in the fourth stanza — was flat…Do I pass?

DAVID: Now — was it very flat – or just a *trifle* — off?

HELENA: What's the difference? Flat is flat — what are you

trying —

DAVID: *Exactly* — flat is flat — ever, ever so slightly flat is flat — off is off — wrong is wrong — you remembered.

HELENA: We are wrong — is that what all this is pointing to?

DAVID: Not we — Yes, *we* — because what affects you affects me.

HELENA: I am wrong.

DAVID: Ever so slightly — yes.

HELENA: I am playing flat.

DAVID: That was the — illustration — you are not flat.

HELENA: I'm *off*.

DAVID: Ever so slightly — you are.

HELENA: Me — *personally?*

DAVID: You…and your —

HELENA: My *music*? My *music* is *off*?

DAVID: Let me tell you a story — years ago, there was a cellist — there *was* a cellist — and there still *is* — I won't state his name — You'd know it — you — well — he progressed in the usual fashion — prodigy — _____ Philadelphia — I won't say which symphony — _____ first chair — and then soloist — He was well received — well respected. And relatively well paid — *and* relatively happy — for a while — then what? The pressure — the celebrity — it started getting to him

— not his ego — not his technique — not his approach — but — something — too much of something — not enough attention — focus — loneliness? In any case, he came to me. It was after a performance of _____. He came to me — "Maestro," he said, "Maestro, I am...unfit" — *Unfit?* He had performed brilliantly — or so it seemed to me — what can an outsider see? Even a conductor — "*In tune with the pulse of each musician*" — his heartbeat — or hers — " [*She touches his hand.*] It's a joke — we're not in tune with anything — the instruments are in tune — the people who bring the instruments to life — I didn't know what each performance was costing him — what resources he was calling upon for each _____ — each — what do they call it on an airplane? — A reserve tank? He was running on his reserve tank. I believe they have them on racing cars — and what happens to racing cars? Well, he was out — his reserve tank was out — his wheels were blown out — he was running on rims — I'm finished, Maestro, he said — I must never attempt to play again — I laughed a comforting laugh — "Rest," I said — "I have rested," he answered. "I have rested two months — since my last concert — and a month before that — rest is not the answer — I am finished." Well, what did he need? He was in perfect health — his concentration was there — the talent...unquestionably — the technique — impeccable — no personal problems — no drugs — alcohol — what then? — I said to him, Berna — [*She seems to recognize name.*] I said to him — step back — not down — do not step down — step back — "Where?" he said — Back, I said — back to the comfort, to the family — take a chair — He was not insulted — he was not shocked — "I don't know if I can even function in a third chair" — Of course you can — step back — He did — I found him a chair in a certain midwestern symphony — my own group was full — a small obscure out-of-the-way — he performed — he supported — he looked to either side of him — he saw friends — he looked straight ahead, he saw someone *else's* behind — ha ha —— sweating — not their behind — they — the soloist — he did *not* sweat — he played — *play* — that's what we begin doing, isn't it? — We *play* the violin — the *fiddle* — like we *play* hide and seek — we *play* — we *play* — and then as we become skilled — the play becomes —

As we become *brilliant* — ha ha — the pressure — to *stay* brilliant — to become *more* brilliant — the competition — the success — notoriety — celebrity — the demands of the public — Manolete — the great Spanish bullfighter — he would let the bull come closer and closer to him until after each naturale — his suit of lights was slightly torn...closer and closer — he said, "They keep wanting more and I have no more to give." Meaning the public...and the critics — and his own need to...surpass — So he gave the — extra inch — and it was — too much — of course — and this was a poor gypsy boy who once used to sneak into pastures at midnight — with an old rag — to *play* with the bulls — *play* — You're not playing, Helena — You are performing — admirably — flawlessly — except for the flat of...what? — Joylessness — You are —

HELENA: I think about *us*—when you love someone — even a musician who loves someone —

DAVID: We can't blame it on love, Helena, love should bring out the best in us — in our art — love should nourish our talent like the rain nourishes a flower — a seed — springing it to life — to full blazing life — colors — petals—leaves

HELENA: Love that is...fading — like a flower — dying —

DAVID: You can't compare music to a flower. Heartbreak can be *heard* — It makes a beautiful sound — loneliness — it stimulates — practice — we turn to our instrument — for solace — comfort — no, Helena — love is the inspiration — unrequited love is the inspiration — loneliness — pain — think of Beethoven's pain — Satie's pain — Chopin — the etudes are written in blood — how many times did Brahms consider suicide? — daily — moment to moment? — Is suicide the answer? It's *an* answer — for some — but only the last answer. First, we try building confidence — Then we try...

HELENA: How can I be confident — as a woman? — I see you looking at me — seeing what? Nothing — seeing me as an instrument — I want to reach out — to touch your hair — to kiss you — all over — It's an embarrassing thing to say.

DAVID: That is why — when one begins to drift away — when one loses the touch — with the music.

HELENA: I do not lose touch. You will not say that to me — No one will say that to me — I hear what I am playing. I mentioned my confidence — as a woman — as a lover? Friend? What am I now? Flautist — but what else? — What am I? What was I ever? Don't answer. But don't question my playing, I *play* — I may not be worth much to you — but I *play*.

DAVID: And that is what I want you to do — my dear, You must play — play again as a child plays — the cellist I mentioned — do you know what happened to him? — After less than a year as a minor role? —You *know* what happened — Everyone knows what happened. Where is he now? — *Ha* — and that's where you will be — you will return refreshed — confident — as — a woman — rested — emotionally — You shall return in triumph — *I* shall conduct you — with the Philharmonic — *with* Rubinstein — I can get him — with Valensky — He'll come out for me —and there you shall be — playing and playing — but playing as you never have before — no, you shall not play music — you shall *be* music — you shall be at one — with me — the orchestra—you shall be *triumphant!* It affects you — it affects your music — and your music affects *me* — It affects me to the extent that I cannot —

HELENA: *Monique* — that was her name — the one I replaced — the cellist — She looks exactly li — it *is* — it *is* Monique —*Monique* — [MONIQUE *nods*] Monique — It is Monique — what is she doing here? — Playing in — I knew she was — your type — you favor those tall, willowy — God — Monique — [*Waves again.*] They're all tall and willowy — that older one— she looks like that photograph of your — [*She realizes.*] It's them — all of them — all your...You've gathered them all to...Background?...Background for what? What are you going to tell me that needs a gathering of old —

DAVID: I have gathered no one.

HELENA: They're playing together — as an ensemble.

DAVID: They *are* an ensemble — they work as an ensemble.

HELENA: Work ?

DAVID: The word unsettles you — work — that is what you do when you have no first chair in my — or anyone else's — symphony — Work — from nine to midnight — without temperament — with or without inspiration — whether or not one is in the mood — whether or not the spirit is in one — one *works* –

HELENA: Temperamental — is that what this — operetta is all about? — A setting to discuss my temperament —

DAVID: I do not discuss.

HELENA: You *say* —You say I am temperamental.

DAVID: Now — yes — during rehearsals — occasionally.

HELENA: During performance — *never* — ever? Ever once — during a performance?

DAVID: During performances is something…else.

HELENA: What else? — What? — My — You're going to harp again on my —

DAVID: I do not harp — harpists harp — cellists cell —

HELENA: Conductors conduct — what are you conducting? Here — What is this composition? — It's all new to me — what *is* this?

DAVID: This is what it is — *this.*

HELENA: What?

DAVID: This…hysteria — this —

HELENA: This hysteria? This is caring, David. This is love — can you —

DAVID: There is a time and a place for love — for — outbursts — not here — and not — on stage.

HELENA: My music is too passionate for the stage? I —

DAVID: *You* — Not your music — You — and you affect me — because I love you — You affect me — my concentration — to look across the brass section — and see two eyes that are interested in you — curious about you — fascinated but demanding — demanding — the best of you — for their continued fascination — that is inspiring — to one's music — one's spirit — but to look over and see — mooning cow eyes — tear-filled cow eyes — an *imploring* in the middle of Debussy — imploring — I feel guilty — nervous — distracted — slightly — slightly, ever so slightly — and the slightest distraction becomes the slightest discomfort, becomes the slightest lack of concentration — becomes the slightest incommunication — becomes the slightest *flaw* in a passage — and I will not have the *slightest* flaw — Adoring — *loving* me — *loving* me — not for the powerful spiritual way that I just brought forth — a perfect crescendo from the kettles and tymps — that is no longer admired or *felt* — eh? Music is insignificant — unheard — unfelt — unplayed — *Love* — *love* — love is fine — nothing interferes with my music... Now what I advise — what I suggest is a — stepping back.

HELENA: To — Seattle?...Minneapolis?

DAVID: Your pride couldn't endure it? It could — it will. It will grow — not pride in — position — pride in humility — and from that — art.

HELENA: Bullshit.

DAVID: Well, you don't have to go. It's just my opinion. What it is worth — you can find another seat in another orchestra — of your choosing — you'll have no trouble — Marlanoff would snap you up in a second — Trilini — Orosco—they'd drool to have you — the little — the almost imperceptible — flaw...If you will — flaw that I find intolerable — they will not notice — or if they do, they will attribute to nervousness — a new orchestra — a new maestro — [*She groans.*] You'll have any seat you choose — any maestro —

HELENA: I don't want a new maestro.

DAVID: Then you shall take the chair I assign you — first or fifth or out in the hall or in the ladies room — in Minneapolis or Timbucktoo. If you find it — advantageous — to your best interests — to play for me — ever again — you shall take the seat I assign you. [*He checks watch.*] Now I'm afraid I must go over some notes — I'm expecting someone.

HELENA: A — cellist?

DAVID: Would you rather I open Friday's program with *no* cellist?

HELENA: And I — step back.

DAVID: If you choose to — if you can — can you? — Or are you so grand — so — dignified — that you can only be supported and never support? Can you support? — Can you humbly — take — what seat? — that one — *there* —

HELENA: With them.

DAVID: *With them* —That is beneath you — with them — they are musicians, goddammit — they are functioning to the limits of their talent — Can you join them? Ha — You've become so big you can't get small...[*He returns back to score.*] I have these notes I must...

HELENA: You...you — couldn't exploit — a woman...two — three-women...even you —

DAVID: Aha — exploitation — some would use the term responsi-bility.

HELENA: To *use* as — as —

DAVID: To place — safely — to continue to function — to...

HELENA: Function.

DAVID: Are they not functioning?

HELENA: For — what? — Background music — for your...

DAVID: *Music* — background — foreground — don't be so damned concerned about what ground you're on or you'll be on no ground at all.

HELENA: *No* ground?

DAVID: You don't believe me? You no longer trust my judgment in these matters ?

HELENA: I trust your *power* — to stop me from ever — to blacklist me from —

DAVID: Ah — blacklist — I will not blacklist you — If you see an — opportunity — take it —

HELENA: Ha ha. What do you want me to do?

DAVID: I want you to live your life. I want your *music to* live.

HELENA: You're asking me to…

DAVID: I'm asking you to *please* let me concentrate on this passage…Some one will join me shortly.

HELENA: [*Stands. looks at trio — looks at him — picks up her instrument — walks to trio — they make room — she sits — she adjusts to group as —*]

[CLAUDIA *enters.*]

CLAUDIA: Am I…?

DAVID: Ah — I've been going over these notes — sit down — please — [*He waves her to seat. Meanwhile,* HELENA *is adjusting to group-one shares music with her — one whispers for a moment with her.*] All right —You're going to play for me — [*She squeals — he silences her with a wave.*] You will play what I say — when I say and how I say — Is that understood? [CLAUDIA *nods.* HELENA *is now playing with the group.*] We open Friday with these three Bartoks and a _____ [*He shoves them at her. She takes them — he pulls them out of her hand and tosses them to floor.*] You know them — this is not a time for study — it is a moment of — what? — Celebration — [*He pours champagne for her.*] To music

CLAUDIA: To — music — [*They drink.*]

DAVID: Good?

CLAUDIA: Perfect — It's a lovely place — [*She glances at quartet.*] It's a lovely group…

LIGHTS FADE

The Scarlet Letter
by Nathaniel Hawthorne
Adapted for the stage by
James F. DeMaiolo

Leslie Fiedler pronounced it the first American tragedy. F.O. Mathiessen considered it the "Puritan Faust." Richard B. Sewall compared its inexorable dramatic force to King Lear. These chieftains of American literature were not, as one might suspect referring to a play by O'Neill. They are not in fact, referring to a play at all, but to a masterpiece of nineteenth century fiction. Until now, it appeared that Nathaniel Hawthorne's haunting drama of judgment, alienation and redemption would be forever confined to the page. The Scarlet Letter continues to be the most frequently read novel in American high schools today as well as one of the most widely circulated novels in the American library system. And now comes the stage version to do it justice.

A century and a half after its first incarnation, James DeMaiolo has forged an alliance of craft and spirit so potent in its own right and so faithful to Hawthorne's original that his stage version is certain to compel all non-believers to recant and take heed. The audience joins the chorus as they weigh the American contract of freedom against the fine print of convention and taboo.

Paper•ISBN 1-55783-243-9 • $6.95
Performance rights available from APPLAUSE

The Day the Bronx Died

A Play
by Michael Henry Brown

"THE DAY THE BRONX DIED COMES ON LIKE
GANGBUSTERS...LIKE A CAREENING SUBWAY
TRAIN spewing its points in a series of breathless
controntations"
—MICHAEL MUSTO, *The New York Daily News*
"Michael Henry Brown is A SMOKING VOLCANO
OF A WRITER...THE DAY THE BRONX DIED is an
engrossin drama... the danger exceeds our expectations"
—JAN STUART, *New York Newsday*

Two childhood friends—one black, the other white—
struggle to live in a racist world.

Michael Henry Brown wrote the screenplay, DEAD
PRESIDENTS directed by the Hughes brothers. He is the
author of the HBO Mini-series LAUREL AVENUE. Among
his other plays is GENERATION OF THE DEAD IN THE
ABYSS OF CONEY ISLAND MADNESS which was
produced to great acclaim at the Long Wharf Theatre in
New Haven and the Penumbra Theatre in St. Paul

Paper•ISBN 1-55783-229-3 • $6.95
Performance rights available from APPLAUSE

BEST AMERICAN SHORT PLAYS 1991-1992

Edited by Howard Stein and Glenn Young

The Best American Short Play series includes a careful mixture of offerings from many prominent established playwrights, as well as up and coming younger playwrights. This collection of short plays truly celebrates the economy and style of the short play form. Doubtless, a must for any library!

Making Contact by **PATRICIA BOSWORTH** • Dreams of Home by **MIGDALIA CRUZ** • A Way with Words by **FRANK D. GILROY** • Prelude and Liebestod by **TERRENCE MCNALLY** • Success by **ARTHUR KOPIT** • The Devil and Billy Markham by **SHEL SILVERSTEIN** • The Last Yankee by **ARTHUR MILLER** • Snails by **SUZAN-LORI PARKS** • Extensions by **MURRAY SCHISGAL** • Tone Clusters by **JOYCE CAROL OATES** • You Can't Trust the Male by **RANDY NOOJIN** • Struck Dumb by **JEAN-CLAUDE VAN ITALLIE** and **JOSEPH CHAIKIN** • The Open Meeting by **A.R.GURNEY**

$12.95 • PAPER • ISBN: 1-55783-113-0 $25.95 • CLOTH• ISBN: 1-55783-112-2

BEST AMERICAN SHORT PLAYS 1990

Salaam, Huey Newton, Salaam by **ED BULLINS** • Naomi in the Living Room by **CHRISTOPHER DURANG** • The Man Who Climbed the Pecan Trees by **HORTON FOOTE** • Teeth by **TINA HOWE** • Sure Ting by **DAVID IVES** • Christmas Eve on Orchard Street by **ALLAN KNEE** • Akhmatova by **ROMULUS LINNEY** • Unprogrammed by **CAROL MACK** • The Cherry Orchard by **RICHARD NELSON** • Hidden in this Picture by **AARON SORKIN** • Boy Meets Girl by **WENDY WASSERSTEIN** • Abstinence by **LANFORD WILSON**

$24.95 CLOTH ISBN 1-55783-084-3 • $12.95 PAPER ISBN 1-55783-085-1

APPLAUSE

BEST AMERICAN SHORT PLAYS 1993-1994

"THE WORK IS FIRST RATE! IT IS EXCITING TO FIND THIS COLLECTON OF TRULY SHORT PLAYS BY TRULY ACCOMPLISHED PLAYWRIGHTS...IDEAL FOR SCHOOL READING AND WORKSHOP PRODUCTIONS:...' —KLIATT

Window of Opportunity by JOHN AUGUSTINE • Barry, Betty, and Bill by RENÉE TAYLOR/JOSEPH BOLOGNA • Come Down Burning by KIA CORTHRON • For Whom the Southern Belle Tolls by CHRISTOPHER DURANG • The Universal Language by DAVID IVES • The Midlife Crisis of Dionysus by GARRISON KEILLOR • The Magenta Shift by CAROL K. MACK • My Left Breast by SUSAN MILLER • The Interview by JOYCE CAROL OATES • Tall Tales from The Kentucky Cycle by ROBERT SCHENKKAN • Blue Stars by STUART SPENCER • An Act of Devotion by DEBORAH TANNEN • Zipless by ERNEST THOMPSON • Date With A Stranger by CHERIE VOGELSTEIN

$15.95 • PAPER • ISBN: 1-55783-199-8 • $29.95 • CLOTH• ISBN: 1-55783-200-5

BEST AMERICAN SHORT PLAYS 1992-1993

Little Red Riding Hood by BILLY ARONSON • Dreamers by SHEL SILVERSTEIN • Jolly by DAVID MAMET • Show by VICTOR BUMBALO • A Couple With a Cat by TONY CONNOR • Bondage by DAVID HENRY HWANG • The Drowing of Manhattan by JOHN FORD NOONAN • The Tack Room by RALPH ARZOOMIAN • The Cowboy, the Indian, and the Fervent Feminist by MURRAY SCHISGAL • The Sausage Eaters by STEPHEN STAROSTA • Night Baseball by GABRIEL TISSIAN • It's Our Town, Too by SUSAN MILLER • Watermelon Rinds by REGINA TALYOR • Pitching to the Star by DONALD MARGULIES • The Valentine Fairy by ERNEST THOMPSON • Aryan Birth by ELIZABETH PAGE

$15.95 • Paper • ISBN 1-55783-166-1 • $29.95 • cloth • ISBN 1-55783-167-X

BEST AMERICAN SHORT PLAYS 1996–1997

Misreadings by NEENA BEEBER • The Rehearsal: A Fantasy by J. RUFUS CALEB • The Vacuum Cleaner by EDWARD de GRAZIA • Mrs. Sorken by CHRISTOPHER DURANG • Four Walls by GUS EDWARDS • I'm With Ya, Duke by HERB GARDNER • My Medea by SUSAN HANSELL • I Didn't Know You Could Cook by RICH ORLOFF • Tunnel of Love by JACQUELYN REINGOLD • Fifty Years Ago by MURRAY SCHISGAL • Your Everyday Ghost Story by LANFORD WILSON • Wildwood Park by DOUG WRIGHT

$15.95 • PAPER • ISBN: 1-55783-317-6 • $29.95 • CLOTH• ISBN: 1-55783-316-8

BEST AMERICAN SHORT PLAYS 1995–1996

Fitting Rooms by SUSAN CINOMAN • Scribe's Paradox or the Mechanical Rabbit by MICHAEL FEINGOLD • Home Section by JANUSZ GLOWACKI • Degas C'est Moi by DAVID IVES • The St. Valentine's Day Massacre by ALLAN KNEE • Old Blues by JONATHAN LEVY • Dearborn Heights by CASSANDRA MEDLEY • When It Comes Early by JOHN FORD NOONAN • American Dreamers by LAVONNE MUELLER • The Original Last Wish Baby by WILLIAM SEEBRING • The Mystery School by PAUL SELIG • The Sandalwood Box by MAC WELLMAN
$15.95 • Paper • ISBN 1-55783-255-2 • $29.95 • cloth • ISBN 1-55783-254-4

BEST AMERICAN SHORT PLAYS 1994–1995

A Stye of the Eye by CHRISTOPHER DURANG • Buck Simple by CRAIG FOLS • Two Mens'es Daughter by J.e. FRANKLIN • An Interview by DAVID MAMET • WASP by STEVE MARTIN • Hot Line by ELAINE MAY • Life Support by MAX MITCHELL • The Whole Shebang by RICH ORLOFF • Dear Kenneth Blake by JACQUELYN REINGOLD • The Cannibal Masque by RONALD RIBMAN • The Artist and the Model by MURRAY SCHISGAL • The Spelling of Coynes by JULES TASCA • The Wreck on the Five-Twenty-Five by THORNTON WILDER • Lot 13: The Bone Violin by DOUG WRIGHT
$15.95 • Paper • ISBN 1-55783-231-5 • $29.95 • cloth • ISBN 1-55783-232-3